HOPE IS DOPE
Achieving Chemical Balance

Steve Treu

Cover design
Randal S. McKenzie

Research Assistant
Madelaine T. Romito

Photos from
iStock

Quantum Revolution Inc.

CRANBERRY TOWNSHIP, PA

Steve Treu/Quantum Revolution Inc.
One Landmark North, Suite 205A
20399 Route 19, Brandt Drive
Cranberry Township, PA/16066
www.qrcounseling.org
www.quantumrevolution.org

Book Layout © 2016 BookDesignTemplates.com

Hope Is Dope/ Steve Treu. -- 1st ed.
ISBN 978-0-9973305-4-0

DEDICATIONS

To Kristen, Austin, Veridy and Aidan
This book is about hope, but I thank you for your patience

To Scott, Larry, Renee, Mike, Teri and Steve
You 'got it' first ... this wouldn't have been done without your support

To Mom and Dad
I'm grateful that hope was always easy to find in our family

To All My Clients
You are both my inspiration and my mirror

To Quantum Revolution Inc.
We will walk the walk as we talk the talk

"If you don't like something, change it.
If you can't change it, change your attitude."
- Maya Angelou

CONTENTS

*"No problem can be solved by the same kind
of thinking that created it."*
– Albert Einstein

L ife doesn't have to feel so difficult.
I promise you, it really doesn't.
It all can change for the better in the blink of an eye
… or in a simple shift of perception.

Most statistics indicate that the United States has reached a
crisis of epic proportions, as drug use continues to skyrocket
despite a *trillion* dollars spent over the past 40 years fighting a
'war' that is being lost. Meanwhile, nearly 20 percent of all
Americans are afflicted with a mental health issue every year,
with the most affected being young adults aged 18-25.

Of course, addiction and mental health issues are closely
related, as they often are co-occurring. The vast majority of
those who are struggling with chemical dependence are also
dealing with depression, anxiety, bipolar disorder, chronic anger
or another emotional disturbance.

This epidemic is an extremely complicated problem that
society has thus far failed to adequately address. This book,
however, will lay out a relatively simple solution that can allow
us to finally be successful.

Putting an end to so much suffering and winning this war
requires us to begin with an essential emotion.

Hope.

It makes all the difference in the world.

First of all, it is logical. Everyone likes hope. No one who feels hopeful rejects it and wishes they could return to hopelessness. No one will argue about the importance of hope, either. It's invaluable and indisputable.

Secondly, it is scientific. Hope is really a 'drug' in itself, a neurochemical cousin to heroin and painkillers. Studies have demonstrated that subjects who take an opioid blocker actually have a hard time feeling hopeful, because the medicine prevents the transmission of that emotion.

Finally, it is practical. We can all be hopeful, as it is readily available. Hope is fuel. It is an energy that motivates us. We are healthier and more productive when we are hopeful. It is also free to produce, needs no prescription, is safe to share with each other, helps us reach our goals and has no adverse side effects. As Einstein's quote suggests, no one solves problems by beating themselves up with negative emotion, which generally created the problems in the first place. But hope is a game-changer.

Hope is chemistry ... and it's cool.

On both levels, hope is truly *dope*!

I have worked with thousands of clients with addiction and mental health issues over the last 15 years. One recurring theme that I have heard has been how depressing many of today's recovery models seem to be. Most clients describe our rehabilitation system as a pretty hopeless industry, despite the best of intentions.

In my opinion, as well as based upon practical experience working with people in the front lines of this war, there is a better way. The human brain is the best physician available to each of us, but most people don't realize that healing literally happens within. The majority of clients that I have worked with have not heard of words such as neurons, neurotransmitters and endorphins. That needs to change.

Fortunately, all we have to do to find hope is learn more about the true nature of the world in which we live. We might also have to be willing to change our perspective a little bit and look inside ourselves rather than outside.

What you 'see' is indeed what you get.

You have to believe you can do it.

We have to believe it can be done.

Discovering hope and all of its benefits does not have to be a complicated search. This book will keep it simple, walking you through many understandable analogies regarding how addiction and mental health issues occur and what to do in order to heal from them.

There is no doubt that mental health disorders and addiction to drugs or alcohol are diseases, especially considering that in both there are cellular changes that lead to a wide range of symptoms and generally include several forms of dysfunction. These diseases create a variety of social, emotional, biological, relational, financial and occupational obstacles.

But there is a cure, which can be defined as the *relief* of the above symptoms and conditions. The antidote to such disease is simply *ease*.

Combatting addiction and mental health issues does not require money as much as it does cultivating an inner sense of *ease* in all of us, both the afflicted and the helpers alike.

That's one reason why I have kept this book relatively short and sweet. I want it to be as easy as possible to understand, so it gets to the point quickly and concisely.

The first section will cover the neuroscientific roots of addiction and mental health issues, using analogies and relatable examples to make otherwise complex information easy enough for a grade school student to comprehend.

The second section will take a look at some pretty cool science that will help us understand who we are ... and why we are the way we are. It borrows a few excerpts from *New Eyes,* my book on the nature of reality, because knowing how you got to where you are can light the pathway toward where you want to go. This section emphasizes that, although we are all so different in many ways, we really are fundamentally very similar, operating under the same set of physical and energetic laws ... albeit from different vantage points. Any insight gained in these chapters not only can inspire hope and perspective, it can help with forgiveness of self and tolerance for others, both key factors in stress reduction and the facilitation of healing.

The third and final section will present the basic strategy for healing, backed by research studies and weaving together the science from the first two parts for a complete package of holistic recovery. Although the neuroscience is not completely settled in all areas, we are in the middle of an epidemic and need to act now. The evidence is compelling — more than a decade of personal experience fighting alongside inspired people has shown me this method works — and we are capable of healing if our attention is focused in the right place.

As such, this book is really more of a manual or a guideline for helping people find their way through their problems to a place of healing.

In contrast to *New Eyes*, which I consider to be a "graduate level" course for clients who are ready for the deepest levels of healing and change, most elements of *Hope is Dope* can be taught to sixth graders. Indeed, most elements of *Hope is Dope* SHOULD be taught to sixth graders!

I teach the scientific concepts within this book in a series of groups; accordingly, much of this information can be used as talking points, teaching tools and conversation starters. There is an entire presentation that goes along with *Hope is Dope,* much of which can be seen online on our YouTube channel (Quantum Revolution Counseling). Quantum Revolution Inc. trains counselors, teachers and administrators to better understand and practice this methodology. We present this information to our clients during dozens of groups and individual counseling sessions, helping them establish healthy habits and train their brains for healing.

Nothing in this book will be too complex. Anyone who is interested will be able to understand it. Healing does not require a graduate degree and therefore should be made as straightforward as possible. In fact, the effectiveness of this modality is in large part due to its simplicity and relatability.

Thankfully, the road to recovery can be a fairly straight path … and the starting line is hope.

1: THE PHARMACY

As bad as the addiction epidemic has become in our country, the good news is that we do not have to travel very far for the solution.

If you are sick and a doctor recommends a certain medicine, where do you go to pick up the prescription?

The local pharmacy.

When it comes to treating addiction as well as many mental health issues, however, often times you need go no further than upstairs.

Into your brain.

That three-pound mass of soft tissue comes loaded with 100 billion little pharmacies called neurons, or nerve cells. Inside of cach neuron are powerful chemicals called neurotransmitters, which are ultimately responsible for our emotional states. It is generally helpful to think of these neurotransmitters as our body's natural drugs.

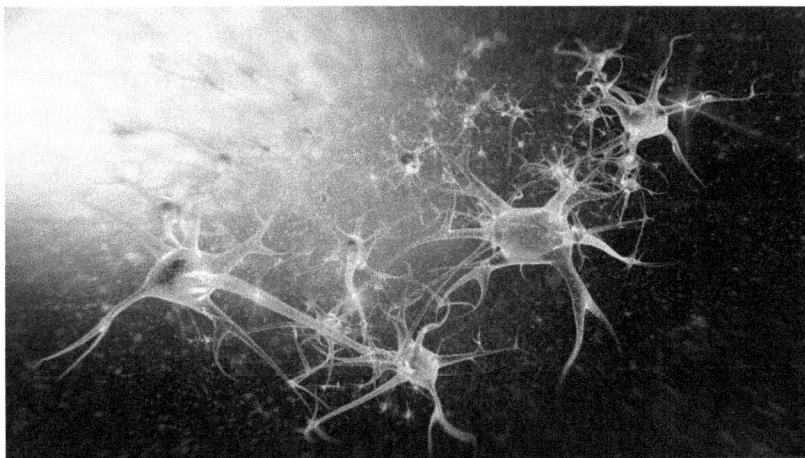

As simple as possible, the structure of a neuron includes:

- Cell body - a neurotransmitter storehouse, much like the shelves within a pharmacy
- Axons - extending out from the body of a nerve cell, axons function like the arm of the pharmacist in that they distribute neurotransmitters within the brain
- Receptors - the part of a neuron that receives a neurotransmitter, much like your hand takes the medicine from the pharmacist
- Synapses - like the counter at a pharmacy, this is the space between the axons and receptors (or between you and the pharmacist) where neurotransmitters are delivered

Neurotransmitter levels are responsible for feelings within our bodies, including emotions such as happiness, depression, relaxation, anxiety and excitement.

Illicit street drugs and psychotropic medicines essentially act as impersonators, 'tricking' the brain into doing things it normally relies on neurotransmitters to do. To be sure, most pharmaceutical drugs are wonderful tools in modern medicine, but they are nevertheless mimics or magnifiers of your body's natural drugs.

For example:

- The brain produces its own opioids in the form of neurotransmitters called endorphins, which fit into endorphin receptors to give the body its pain-relieving effects. Turns out that heroin and pain-killing pills also fit into those receptors, intensifying the feeling that endorphins ('endogenous morphine') typically provide.
- Cocaine, methamphetamine and other stimulants work by elevating levels of dopamine in the brain. The cocaine itself is not what makes one feel high, it is the excessive amount of dopamine in the brain. Cocaine

merely clogs up the receptor sites, forcing dopamine to pin-ball within the synapse for an artificial effect. It is the dopamine that is responsible for excitement and awareness. Dopamine is also produced in high amounts with other substances as users become excited in anticipation of, and during, their high.

• Benzodiazepines and alcohol merely enhance the effectiveness of GABA, or gamma-aminobutyric acid, which inhibits nerve transmission and reduces anxiety. GABA is the reason why medicines such as Valium and Xanax, along with alcohol, 'take the edge off' of someone who is feeling stress.

• Antidepressants such as Prozac and Paxil attempt to boost the brain's serotonin levels, which when low are equated with depression. The 'trip' associated with the use of psychedelics such as LSD has been associated with the elevation of serotonin as well.

• Marijuana resembles the neurotransmitter anandamide, which is derived from the Sanskrit word 'ananda' meaning 'bliss.' The blissful high that marijuana users experience stems from the activation of cannabinoid receptors.

This means that all of us have a potential chemical cocktail of good feelings inside of our brains in the presence of endorphins, dopamine, GABA, serotonin and anandamide.

It means that heroin, painkillers, cocaine, alcohol, sedative pills, antidepressants and marijuana are all available for production in their 'natural' form by anyone who wishes to seek them.

It means that anyone struggling with addiction and mood disorders or other mental health issues have the best available medicine for treatment right inside their own minds.

There is a pharmacist living up there who shares your name, because YOU are the manager of your own natural pharmacy.

To be clear, medicine can be a very valuable tool in health and healing. Physicians and pharmacists should always be consulted on relevant medicinal matters.

But to rely solely on medicine to solve problems is short-sighted and frustrating for many people. Hope is dope because hope is found in your brain, along with many other wonderful virtues and their neurochemical counterparts.

Seek help when you need help … both from the outside world and the one within.

2: HIJACKING

W e all like to be in control.
    Whether it is managing our lives or driving a car, a sense of direct influence over the direction we are going is essential to happiness.

It's why so many people are derailed by addiction and mental health problems, which wrest that sense of control away and make us feel as if we have been hijacked, for good reason.

That is almost exactly what happens in our brains.

By definition, a hijacking is when something takes control of something else by force. Well, drugs *are* thugs. They beat us up and commandeer our brains. Once they get in, they steal many things, including one of our most valuable possessions — a sense of empowerment.

Neurotransmitters fit into receptors just as keys fit into locks. The shape of the key has to be the right match in order to open the lock. If the shape is different, the key will not work.

Drugs happen to be shaped in a similar fashion to the neurotransmitters that they mimic. In general, they fit into the same locks, which is why they work. They 'turn on' the receptors and create the effect that the neurotransmitters do, though typically much more intensely.

Heroin, for example, has nearly the exact same shape as methadone, OxyContin and Vicodin. They all are comprised of similar amounts of carbon, hydrogen, nitrogen and oxygen, therefore their chemical formulas are only slightly different:

- Heroin - $C_{21} H_{23} N O_5$
- Methadone - $C_{21} H_{27} N O$
- OxyContin - $C_{18} H_{21} N O_4$
- Vicodin - $C_{18} H_{21} N O_3$
- Morphine - $C_{17} H_{19} N O_3$

See how chemically similar they all are? Accordingly, they are practically the same 'key' that happens to have the same 'shape' to fit into the endorphin receptor 'lock.'

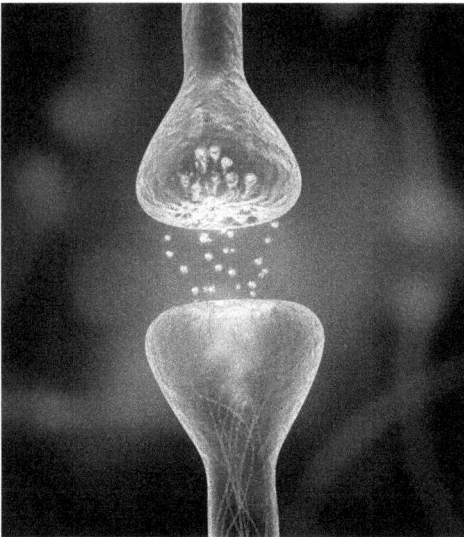

It's like a Trojan Horse, as the brain is 'tricked' into operating as if an endorphin molecule has entered the receptor when really it is an opioid.

There is a natural consequence to this 'deception.' In the process one of two things occur, either the upregulation (increase) or the downregulation (decrease) in the amount of receptors.

It's sort of like food going into a stomach, which expands and contracts depending upon the amount consumed. If someone overeats the stomach gets bigger … and over time this leads to an increase in hunger as a larger stomach size sends signals to a person to eat more. Alternatively, if someone deprives themselves of food, the stomach shrinks and less food is ultimately needed to fill it.

With chemical dependence, increased receptor availability (upregulation) also sends a message to a person to use more. This is called *craving* and it is extremely difficult to ignore, much like it is nearly impossible to distract oneself from the hunger pangs of an empty stomach. The receptors, like an empty stomach, start screaming inside your head, "Feed Me!" All addicts recognize the hijacker's voice inside of their head and find it virtually impossible to say no to its demands, in spite of what everyone on the outside is saying. Try as they might, they cannot get that voice to be quiet. They feel as if they are being held at gunpoint inside their own minds.

Many studies demonstrate that this is exactly what happens with the use of heroin and painkillers, as a greater amount of endorphin receptors creates a desire to use more drugs while also creating an ability to do so, called tolerance. The problem is compounded by the activation of the brain's reward system in the ventral tegmental area, producing an overflow of reinforcing dopamine that also stimulates the addict to use more.

Others drugs cause downregulation, and decreased receptor availability makes it difficult to feel certain emotions in much the same way it would be hard to eat a lot with a very small stomach. In specific, cocaine use reduces the number of dopamine receptors, which makes it hard to feel excitement even when something interesting is going on because there is nowhere for dopamine to go. (Imagine trying to eat without a mouth to put food in. That's hard to do.) Often, this results in depression due to prevailing boredom and a lack of motivation, leading to a downward spiral of increased use that is sometimes called "chasing the dragon," when users repeatedly seek an elusive high but can never quite find it since the brain's receptors have been significantly altered.

The science is not entirely conclusive regarding upregulation vs. downregulation of certain receptors, but either way the effect is the same — drugs have hijacked the brain and take control. They dictate behaviors to a large extent because the emotional system is compromised and a desire to use is increased while simultaneously triggering feelings of sadness, boredom and stress. Those emotions are cues to engage in certain behaviors, especially using more drugs, and the sick cycle continues.

It is not that different with depression or anxiety, as receptor sensitivities are affected over time and a person's own mind plays the role of the hijacker. "Stinking thinking" and worrisome thoughts generate a negative neurochemical avalanche, leading to another dysfunctional brain change that will be discussed in the next section.

Once those receptors have been altered, a person no longer feels in charge because a hijacker has commandeered the brain.

This is why society needs to show patience and understanding while withholding judgment. Does anyone think a person who hasn't eaten for three days is weak for thinking of food? Does anyone blame a hijacking victim for feeling anxious and taking a few wrong turns? Of course not. We need to encourage people not to try drugs in the first place, for sure, but once the hijacker is in the car … the driver tends to lose control.

Thankfully, there are excellent methods to eject the hijacker and resume command in our lives again.

3: HIBERNATION

Understanding the primary problem in addiction and mood disorders merely requires grasping a simple fact of life within the animal kingdom.

What does a bear do when it is hibernating?

That's right, virtually nothing. It is alive, but inactive. It might even stir a little bit, but a bear will remain very sluggish until it fully wakes up again. It's in a deep sleep.

Now you can visualize the problem — as well as the solution — for chemical dependence, depression, anxiety, toxic anger and more.

When using drugs or when struggling emotionally, the root physical cause is hibernating neurotransmitters.

The body responds to drug use by lulling the brain's natural counterparts to sleep. The best example of this is with heroin, which is such a powerful hijacker that endorphins are knocked unconscious, so to speak. It is actually the body's way of trying to restore sanity, as there is no need for the brain to produce endorphins if someone is loading up with 'fake' endorphins instead.

With endorphins becoming inactive, the active heroin user is left with nothing to fill those receptors except for more heroin!

Combined with an increased amount of receptors, the craving is so intense that the addict can practically think of nothing else.

Once again, think of anyone who goes a few days without food ... they typically can think of nothing else other than the desire to fill the stomach, either. It's what makes quitting the use of heroin so difficult, because those "Feed Me!" thoughts are especially intense while the endorphins are asleep. The opioid addict seemingly has only one alternative to feel better: more opioids.

It's why the most hopeful way to characterize a person who is chemically dependent upon heroin or painkillers is as someone with a *hibernating endorphin* syndrome.

To only pay attention to the damaging effects of the drug takes the focus off the real underlying physiological problem, which is the resulting chemical imbalance, and keeps us from focusing on how to actually succeed in recovery.

In the case of opioid addiction, this is done by waking up those endorphins.

Similarly, repeated use of cocaine and marijuana lead to the downregulation of natural dopamine and anandamide production, respectively, which is why users of those drugs lack motivation without the use of the chemical — or even with it. They need the drug to play the role that the neurotransmitters are supposed to be playing.

Excessive worrying leads to the hibernation of GABA, or the body's natural sedative. Chronic use of benzodiazepines (Valium, Xanax, Klonopin) leads to a decrease of GABA receptors and GABA functioning. The solution is to stir GABA out of hibernation using a variety of mental and physical techniques.

Maladaptive thoughts or negative self-talk leads to the hibernation of serotonin, or the body's natural happiness chemical. Similar to what happens with anxiety and GABA, when serotonin goes to sleep in the brain, a person reports feeling depressed. The solution is to wake up that serotonin.

Studies have demonstrated that dopamine, GABA and serotonin may all be involved in bipolar disorder. Not surprisingly, as drugs are introduced to the brain when someone has a mental health issue, the chemistry gets even more complex.

But there is an easy way to think about these issues.

It's by thinking differently about how to approach treatment.

We have a name for what happens in the brain during addiction or depression — *chemical imbalance.*

There is a simple name for the cure — *chemical balance.*

The problem is imbalance and the solution is balance.

Hijackers and hibernators hate balance. Happy, healthy people have to be balanced.

4: DEBT

While not easy to do, losing weight is easy to understand.

Burn more calories than you consume and typically you will lose weight.

Similarly, falling into financial debt is easy to comprehend as well.

Spend more money than you earn and you will fall into debt.

If I make $50,000 in a year and I spend $70,000, I am $20,000 in debt. Credit card companies and banks generally tend to keep track of such debts, so that 20 grand is not likely to disappear on its own anytime soon. Those lenders will eventually come knocking.

It is the same way in the brain.

Once a chemical imbalance occurs through either excessive drug use or maladaptive thought patterns, a similar type of debt occurs. Addiction and mental health issues all typically involve a neurological debt, with neurotransmitters representing money earned and the receptors representing money spent or money owed.

Sometimes, as with opioid addiction, this is a perfect comparison. When someone uses 'imitation' endorphins in the form of heroin or painkillers, doing so is like borrowing on credit and therefore a debt is incurred. The receptor 'banks' will demand payment, but there is no healthy way to satisfy them since the real money (endorphins) is hibernating.

When someone tries to stop using drugs, the receptors still want to be 'fed' just as the financial lenders still want to be paid … so now we have an *endorphin debt*.

The solution? Well, if you want to get out of financial debt, you have to generate more money to pay off those creditors. If you want to get out of endorphin debt, you have to create more endorphins to satisfy those receptors.

In each case, you must stop that excessive spending that led to the problem in the first place. In financial matters, this means to stop unnecessary spending. In addiction, this means to stop using drugs. With mental health issues, it requires a change in thinking patterns.

But does stopping or even curtailing spending solve the financial problem? No, because the debt will remain if you don't pay back the lender by making more money.

Same with addiction. Does abstinence from drugs solve the chemical dependence? No, because as long as those endorphins are hibernating, those receptors will be craving.

This is why relapse occurs so often, because most people blame the drug as the primary problem without fully addressing the chemical imbalance that lies underneath. When someone stops using, over time the receptors naturally restore themselves to baseline, but the addict remembers the pleasurable feeling and often continues to have urges to use if that debt is not paid and chemical balance is not restored.

In the addiction community this is often termed 'white knuckle' recovery, when someone is 'holding on for dear life' while not using. They may be abstinent, but do not feel much better for it. Similarly, the slang term 'dry drunk' is what someone experiences when they are not drinking alcohol but still have most of the dysfunction of someone who has been abusing it.

That is because stopping using drugs or being abstinent from alcohol is only part of the solution, whereas waking up sleeping neurotransmitters makes it so much easier to succeed.

Most forms of addiction and mental health challenges fit right into this model.

Alcoholics and benzodiazepine abusers experience a form of GABA debt, similar to someone with anxiety. Marijuana users experience a form of anandamide debt, which is why they get irritable when their natural 'joy' or 'bliss' brain chemicals are inactive.

People suffering from depression have a serotonin debt — indeed, antidepressants are commonly described as a way of dealing with a chemical imbalance by artificially increasing the amount of serotonin available in the synapse. This is similar to offering someone with money problems a loan consolidation or extending them another line of credit. That can certainly be helpful, but is not an effective long-term solution if serotonin is not produced naturally again.

Solutions to all of the above include stopping the spending (using drugs, drinking alcohol, excessive worrying, negative self-talk) and making more money (endorphins, dopamine, GABA, serotonin, anandamide).

That is the complete approach to healing: Abstinence from drugs and alcohol combined with a healthy mind that wakes up sleeping neurotransmitters, restoring chemical balance.

The disease fades away over time when you are *at ease*.

5: CRUTCHES

If you break a leg and get a cast, what's one of your most important possessions for the next eight weeks? *Your crutches.*

Are crutches good for you? *Of course! They allow you time to heal.*

Are they a 'substitute' for your actual leg? *Absolutely! Your leg is broken and is not capable of carrying its weight, so the crutches carry the burden for a while.*

What is their medical role? *Crutches provide support for you while you heal.*

Do they ever take the place of your actual leg? *Of course not! As long as your leg is capable of healing, no one is satisfied with hobbling around on crutches.*

When your leg heals, what do you do with the crutches? *You stop using them.*

Now you understand the role of medicine in addiction and mental health.

Medicine is a crutch. And there is absolutely nothing wrong with using medicine, as long as it is used properly.

Can crutches for a broken leg be used improperly? Sure, jogging or punting footballs with a broken leg is a pretty bad idea. You can also use crutches that are too big for you or too small, which will make you unstable. And using crutches only when you feel like it is also a bad idea, such as not walking with them on Tuesdays and Thursdays for some reason.

Medicine is precisely like that. You can use it incorrectly, but that's not the fault of the medicine. You can use too much medicine or too little. You can use it only when you feel like it, which is also a bad idea and often leads to complications.

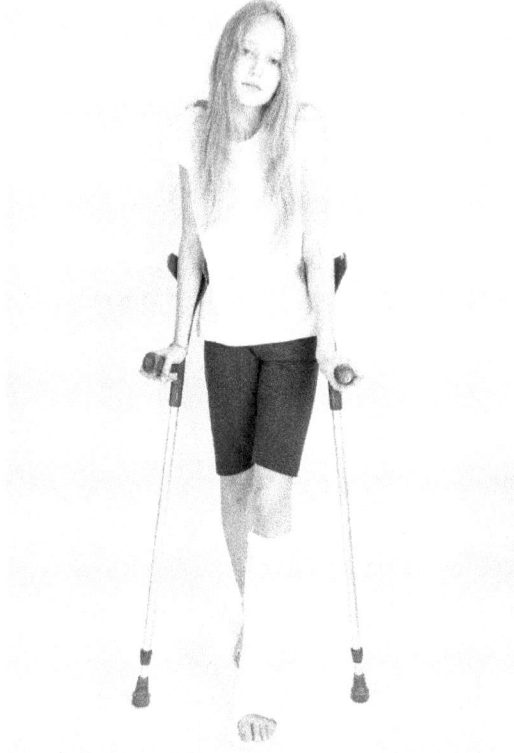

When used correctly, however, medicine is a very valuable tool. It offers support while you get better, helping your brain function well enough to make progress toward recovery and healing.

There are a wide variety of prescription pharmaceuticals that work well for many people seeking treatment, including antidepressants, sedatives, opioid medicines, mood stabilizers, alcohol blockers and several more.

All of them are useful when used appropriately and when they are individualized. Just as crutches need to be bigger for a taller person and smaller for a shorter person, doses and different types of medicine must 'fit' the patient correctly.

There is a proper way to stop using medicines, too. Just as you don't start running immediately as your leg begins to heal, you typically need to taper off prescriptions so that you do not get 're-injured' or relapse. You should proceed with caution.

But do the crutches actually heal anything? No, *they just give you the opportunity to heal yourself.*

In the case of opioid medicines such as buprenorphine and methadone, they occupy endorphin receptors for at least 24 hours so that cravings for heroin and painkillers subside for a while. Antidepressants merely inhibit reuptake so that serotonin pinballs around in the synapse, but a user of that medicine doesn't necessarily produce any more of their own 'happiness' serotonin in the process. Sedatives reduce anxiety by playing the role of GABA, which acts like the brakes on a car to slow the stressful traffic in the brain, though once again the user of that medicine has not generated a release of their own relaxing GABA.

See the benefit ... and the dilemma?

The medicines are doing the work, which allows you an opportunity to feel better and take action to heal yourself. But if you do nothing and the meds are removed, the hijacker jumps right back inside the car.

Bottom line: medicine helps those who help themselves.

Unfortunately many people tend to rely on medicinal crutches forever, believing them to be absolutely necessary. In some cases that may be true, but most meds are not needed for a lifetime. Can you imagine breaking your leg and then using crutches for the next 30 years?

As discussed in the first four chapters, healing happens in the brain through restoring chemical balance.

An opioid addict must wake up their hibernating endorphins again.

A cocaine addict must find other ways to produce dopamine.

A marijuana user must generate their own anandamide in order to quit.

An alcoholic and benzodiazepine user must create higher levels of GABA, similar to someone who has an anxiety disorder.

Those with depression or bipolar disorder benefit from the

balancing of serotonin in their systems.

The next time anyone says that using medicine to treat addiction or mental health issues is a substitute, ask them this: Is using crutches for a broken leg a substitute?

You bet it is. And it is a smart one ... if used properly.

6: THE JUMPSTART

It's a dark and stormy night.

You are stranded on the side of the road and your car won't start.

All you want to hear from any kindly stranger who drives by are those three magic words.

"Need a jump?"

After you gratefully accept — and after the jumper cables are connected between the alive and the dead batteries — your car's engine fires right up again.

It's also the first step in turning around the life of someone who has been struggling with addiction and mental health.

They need a jumpstart.

The problem for whatever ails them is chemical imbalance and the solution to that problem is chemical balance. Easier said than done, for sure, but many people do not realize that the healing answers to their aching questions are found within.

Although we often refer to car batteries as dead, the truth is they are just lacking the requisite 'healthy' energy. That's the same with our brains when we are depressed, anxious or addicted to drugs or alcohol.

The most important thing to do in this situation is provide a jumpstart to our neurons, jolting those hibernating neurotransmitters back into action. This means making some changes. You can't start a fire without a spark.

Above all else, knowledge is power — and science demonstrates that healing is possible.

If you are suffering from addiction or mental health issues, there is plenty of hope. Your brain comes equipped with all the medicine you need to cure yourself. Just knowing that healing is possible can be enough of a jumpstart. Be hopeful. Talk hopefully. Behave hopefully.

Hope produces endorphins!

When someone is addicted or depressed and they receive a jolt of endorphins from their own mind, clearly it feels good and increases the likelihood of changing behaviors while decreasing the probability of dysfunction. This can be enough to get the ball rolling in recovery.

Accordingly, if you are a family member, friend, teacher or counselor of someone in this situation, the most important thing you can do is believe in their ability to succeed. Shame, guilt and threats are terrible motivators, but hopefulness, optimism and encouragement are excellent jumpstarters. Cultivating these positive emotions can activate the brain's reward system (that has been compromised by drug abuse) by producing dopamine, which chemically reinforces healthy moods. It's important to boost dopamine levels naturally by getting *excited* about recovery.

Hope can provide that spark and can be contagious, spreading throughout the brain — and throughout a community — like a campfire lights up when enough kindling ignites. (We will go over the science of this phenomenon in Chapter 17.)

Also coming up, we will reveal dozens of proven ways to fan the neurotransmitter flames in our brains to bring about whole recovery.

Consider Albert Einstein's quote again:

> *"No problem can be solved by the same kind of thinking that created it."*

Another way of saying that is this:

> *"You cannot start the engine of a car with a dead battery."*

When your mind begins to burn with belief in healing, everything heats up for the better. Getting an optimistic jumpstart is required to get that sluggish brain back up and running. If the brain doesn't wake up, crutches often seem to be useless and relapse becomes common.

If you or someone you know is struggling, feeling bad about it isn't going to help much. Our society has become addicted to negativity and pessimism. That is not healing anyone. Ever try to start a campfire with wet sticks? It gets smoky, at best.

Inspiration, however, does heal. It lights that fire. Shift your mindset toward something true and encouraging so that you can feel the positive effects.

Our brains have the ability to change. Once brains change, emotions and behaviors change. Millions and millions of people have reversed the dysfunctional effects of addiction and mental health issues — we should focus on how they did it.

It's called chemical balance. Everyone can do it.

What you believe, you can achieve.

7: THE BUTTERFLY EFFECT

It doesn't take much to turn a life around.

Does it require gaining fame or popularity? *Nope.*

Winning a championship or the lottery? *Not necessary.*

Falling in love, getting a scholarship, buying a home and being elected president or homecoming queen? *No, no, no and no.*

Dramatically changing the direction of one's life is much simpler than all of the above.

All it takes is a flap of a butterfly's wing.

Seriously. (And metaphorically.)

Half a century ago, when computers were in their infancy, a meteorologist by the name of Edward Lorenz began using the fancy new gadget to try to improve weather forecasting models.

Lorenz pumped a whole bunch of weather data — things like temperature, barometric pressure, dew point, etc. — into

computers and carefully studied the results. At one point he reran a computer simulation with precisely the same numbers he had done before, save for one minor detail.

One model had the number .506 as a piece of data and the other .506127 in the same spot. In effect, one computer model had a wee little bit more wind velocity than the other.

At first, the systems produced the exact same prognostications, as you would anticipate. But over a two-month period of time, something dramatic that you wouldn't expect happened.

What was going to be a sunny day, according to one computer simulation, morphed into a rainy day on the other.

Just by altering one insignificant piece of data by .000127 the whole projection changed significantly.

A decade later at a major scientific conference, after this mathematical phenomenon had been retested and definitively verified, Lorenz gave a speech that a colleague entitled, "Does the Flap of a Butterfly's Wings in Brazil set off a Tornado in Texas?"

The Butterfly Effect was born.

Tiny little changes can lead to great big changes.

At the start of the Ashton Kutcher movie *The Butterfly Effect*, this quote appears: "It has been said that something so small as the flutter of a butterfly's wing can ultimately cause a typhoon halfway around the world."

In the movie, every time the protagonist makes a change, the future is radically altered. In effect, that's the Butterfly Effect.

For anyone with depression, anxiety or addiction issues, there may no scientific concept more important than this one. It's the science of a jumpstart.

Every journey starts with one step. While the weight of chemical dependence and mental health burdens might be heavy, it can change drastically by merely beginning the walk toward recovery with confidence.

Each little effort someone makes today in order to alter the course of their lives adds a little wind to their sails. Just imagine what a million flapping butterflies can do!

Problems persist when there is no change — no flap of a

butterfly's wing — and symptoms continue for days, weeks, months and sometimes years. It becomes very robotic, and like a robot, leaves people feeling empty inside.

This book will describe dozens of ways to fly. You don't have to do much at first, just a little bit is enough.

A little change today can morph into a lot of happiness tomorrow.

8: RELATIVITY

The world is not what we think it is.

Albert Einstein developed a theory a century ago that has stood the test of time, and when we apply it to our lives, it has amazing implications.

In a nutshell, Einstein's Theory of Relativity states that the speed of light is always the same and neither space nor time is constant. What that means is that the physical world is *different* for each person, as everyone has his or her own individual relationship with the universe.

We tend to think that the world is constant, that it is 'out there' … but relativity and another scientific concept called the observer effect (Chapter 10) have demonstrated that the world is really more 'in here' (inside of us) than anything else.

What we think of as space and time is really just one thing that Einstein termed *spacetime*, which includes a pair of effects called length contraction and time dilation. The simplistic bottom line of these concepts is that an object *changes size* depending on whom is looking at it, while time can pass at *different* rates of speed.

Understanding the complicated science of this is really challenging — and also not necessary. All you need to know is that spacetime is *flexible*, in effect 'altering' itself for each of us individually based upon the way we each are observing it.

Relativity is a reality-shifting concept, as well as a perfect metaphor for tolerance and for understanding each other.
Since we all have our own unique relationship with the universe, it means that we are all experiencing the world in our

own personalized way, which means that none of us really has the right to definitively judge another person's point of view!

It's all *relative*, so it's all a matter of perspective.

One way to visualize this is by thinking about mice in a maze, sniffing for the cheese at the exit. One mouse is placed in a difficult spot, around many corners, far from the cheese. Obstacles abound, including dark alleys where painful traps are set. Meanwhile, another mouse is placed near the exit, by the cheese, with nary an obstacle in sight.

Will the mice have different journeys to get to their destination? Of course. Is one mouse 'better' than the other because he had it easier? Of course not. Can the mouse placed in the difficult situation actually learn more by going through adversity? Definitely!

Life is like that. Some people are born near the cheese, others far from it. But the objective is the same, the one desire we all have in common … to be happy. And that's done by balancing brain chemistry.

As the theory of relativity suggests, we each have our own unique perspective, which means we each have different angles from which we approach life. For example, some people need to learn how to speak up for themselves while others need to learn how to stop talking about themselves. Some people would benefit by being more forgiving, with others needing to be less enabling.

The list goes on and on. For every person who needs to work on being courageous, there is someone who needs to take fewer dangerous risks. For every person who would benefit by taking life less seriously and developing their sense of humor, there is someone who needs to practice discipline and stop being such a class clown.

It's all relative.

Interestingly enough, thanks to Einstein's relativity, the world appears to 'change' along with us as we change ourselves from the inside. In quantum physics, the observer effect suggests that when we look at situations differently, it is probable that the situation changes as well.

This is another reason why hope is so important. Just believing that change is possible begins to create conditions for healing.

Your job is to figure out what change might be necessary in your life without comparing yourself to others, because everyone has something different to work on in order to create chemical balance and peace in their lives.

9: EVERYTHING IS ENERGY

We have all heard of $E = mc^2$, but do we all know what it really means?

Albert Einstein himself didn't think we would. He said of his famous equation, "Mass and energy are both but different manifestations of the same thing — a somewhat unfamiliar conception for the average mind."

Hope Is Dope is all about people having exceptionally balanced minds, so let's make $E = mc^2$ a familiar conception!

The "E" stands for energy and the "m" represents mass with "c^2" equating to the speed of light squared. Understanding it can be complex, so we will keep it simple by emphasizing the essential part of Einstein's quote:

"Mass and energy are both but different manifestations of the same thing."

Mass is stuff. Energy is non-stuff. And Einstein said that stuff and non-stuff are really made of the same stuff!

On the surface, $E = mc^2$ indicates how much energy anything with mass has, simply illustrated by the nuclear bomb. It essentially means that if you mess with mass a whole lot, a whole lot of energy gets released. Once Einstein figured out the equation, it was only a matter of time before the nuclear bomb was created. All the energy that destroyed Hiroshima in World War II came from about two pounds of enriched uranium inside the bomb.

But if we dig deeper, $E = mc^2$ ultimately means that *everything* is made up of energy. The sun, the stars, this table, that ham sandwich, music, puppies, your mind, your brain, your right thumb, emotions, baseballs, tutus, Pokemon, you … everything is energy! As we shall see, that's a very big deal.

One quick way to understand that concept is to consider H_2O. In liquid form, it is H_2O. In solid form, it is H_2O. That means water and ice are "different manifestations of the same thing."

Another way of understanding it is this: Take a tree, cut it in half. What do you have? Two halves of a tree.

Now chop those halves into halves. What do you have? Yep, quarters of a tree.

Now keep chopping. You have a bunch of 2x4-sized tree parts. More chopping, smaller pieces of the tree. Down to sticks, then toothpicks, then sawdust. A huge mound of sawdust.

So what if you keep cutting the sawdust in half?

Well, reduce anything down to its constituent parts and you reach the level of molecules, which are composed of atoms, which when I was younger I conceptualized to be just smaller parts of the original tree.

But that's far from the facts! On the atomic level, the tree stops being a tree, much like a cookie isn't a cookie prior to mixing the butter, sugar, flour and eggs together. Just as similar parts that make up a cookie can go instead to making a cake, similar parts that make up a tree also make up other things.

Wood is comprised largely of carbon, oxygen and hydrogen. You know what else is also comprised largely of carbon, oxygen and hydrogen? Your body. Yeah, that's right, increase the amount of carbon in your body from 19 percent to 50 percent, decrease the amount of oxygen from 65 percent to 44 percent and tweak the amount of hydrogen by removing a bit and presto chango … you just became Pinocchio.

And that's no lie!

Like cookies and cakes or human bodies and wood, physical matter is all about how you combine the same basic atomic ingredients into different forms.

We can dig even deeper, as atoms are comprised of electrons, protons and neutrons. Those particles are made up of even smaller particles of things like quarks, leptons and bosons. Included somewhere in that mass of stuff are gluons, which help 'glue' it all together. This is the quantum level, and we are almost done being able to reduce that tree.

With math, you can keep cutting numbers in half. Start with the number 16, cut it to 8, now 4, then 2, and so on, for infinity.

With matter, this is not so. You cannot keep chopping it in half. You eventually reach a limit, or a scale that is called "Planck length" after the man (Max Planck) who figured out that things could only get so small before they hit a wall of no-thingness.

Keep cutting sawdust in half and eventually you reach:
.00000000000000000000000000000001616199 of a meter

In standard notion it is 1.616199×10^{-35} and in standard language it is "impossible to ever see."

Take a piece of sawdust and cut it into a trillion pieces. Then cut that trillionth of a piece into a trillion pieces. Repeat one more time and you're there … Planck length. This is the scale beyond which our normal idea of size becomes incomprehensible, as shorter lengths do not make physical sense. Basically it would be like trying to measure the size of zero. That does not compute.

It is down here in the world of the infinitesimally small where we reach our ultimate destination of understanding the importance of $E = mc^2$. Using math and physics, some scientific

geniuses have reduced a trillionth of a trillionth of a trillionth of a piece of sawdust and discovered ... your mind!

Well, not quite, but close enough for our purposes. Your mind comes from the interaction between your brain and special type of energy called consciousness. Without consciousness, there is no mind. But with consciousness, mind rises up through the brain and we have mental experiences.

"I regard consciousness as fundamental," said Planck in 1931. "I regard matter as derivative from consciousness. We cannot get behind consciousness."

In essence, this means that your mind is a very, very important thing in changing our lives. When we deconstruct the physical world, we are only left with our minds.

Everything is relative and everything is energy. In the next chapter you will see how that mental energy runs your life.

10: THE OBSERVER EFFECT

Have you ever played golf and stood over a tee shot on a Par-3 hole with a water hazard in front of you? During your backswing, if you are thinking about the lake, what's likely to happen to the ball? Yep, all wet.

When an opponent is shooting a free throw, why do the home fans at basketball games attempt to distract him? Because if it changes the shooter's focus, it works.

If a teenage boy is going to ask his crush out on a date for the first time, is she more or less likely to say 'yes' if he is confident … or if he seems insecure, with his head down, kicking at the dirt? Same with a job interview, all else equal, doesn't a person who presents with healthy self-esteem stand a better chance at being hired?

Or how about this: There once was a long train that asked to be pulled over a high mountain. None of the big engines were up to the task, but when asked if he could do it, the Little Engine replied, "I think I can."

It was an arduous chore indeed! Struggling to get up a high peak, the Little Engine repeated his mantra to himself, "I think I can, I think I can, I think I can."

Sure enough, he did it. He got the train over the big hill and basked in his success, "I thought I could! I thought I could!

Although that story is make-believe, parents have been reading it to children for nearly a century now. Why? Because it's based in truth!

There is no historical accuracy to *The Little Engine That*

Could ... just tons of anecdotal evidence and plenty of research that supports the moral of the story. There's science behind confidence.

It's called the observer effect.

The way you look at things affects those things.

The observer effect started with something called the double-slit experiment. You can see excellent explanations of this on the internet by searching for "dr. quantum double slit experiment" (from the eye-opening *What The Bleep!?: Down The Rabbit Hole* movie) or "the original double slit experiment" (by Veritasium, a superb science site).

Originally conceptualized by Thomas Young in 1801, the double-slit experiment has since been replicated, analyzed, re-analyzed and reformulated in countless numbers of ways, including the Delayed-Choice Experiment and the Quantum Eraser, until it has been proven to be the way quantum things work. It's also how most, if not all, things in the universe work.

And here's how things work, as simple as possible.

Light, which is responsible for everything we see and makes all of our experiences possible, travels as both waves and particles. It is a wave when you are not directly 'observing' it and it becomes a particle when you directly 'observe' it.

In other words, similar to time dilation and length contraction in relativity, light and sub-atomic particles behave differently depending upon what you are doing. According to some of the most brilliant people ever to walk the face of the earth, the world is 'reacting' to the manner in which you look at it. It's as if the physical world is 'watching' you, too.

"If we consider what matter really is, we now understand it as much more of a mathematical thing ... I think that matter itself is now much more of a mental substance."

-   Sir Roger Penrose,
mathematical physics professor at the University of Oxford

Penrose is a really smart guy. His comment that "matter is more of a mental substance" is similar to Planck saying, "I regard matter as derivative from consciousness."

And one more for good measure — physicist Niels Bohr said, "Everything we call real is made of things that cannot be regarded as real."

That is so important, you should read it again: "Everything we call real is made of things that cannot be regarded as real."

That's because everything is energy, not matter, and all that energy (and apparent matter) is being affected by our minds.

Medically, this explains the placebo effect. A placebo is a 'fake' medicine or procedure and a placebo effect is when a treatment using a placebo benefits the patient in a way that cannot be attributed to any medicine or procedure, therefore must be due to the patient's beliefs or expectations.

What the observer effect clearly indicates is that you can *influence* the prognosis of an addiction or a mental health issue (or a golf shot or job interview, etc.) by what's going through your mind.

Confidence matters. Belief matters. Expectation matters. Imagination matters. Because as Penrose suggested, matter is really just a form of confidence, belief, expectation and imagination.

"With imagination," said imaginary philosopher SpongeBob SquarePants, "I can be anything I want."

And that's pretty close to the truth.

This is eminently clear in addiction treatment. If clients believe what they have been told far too often — that they have an incurable disease and are likely to relapse because statistics demonstrate that — then that is precisely what tends to happen.

We don't want people contemplating, "I think I can't, I think I can't."

The mind affects the body. Confidence, belief, expectation and imagination matter. If you can see it in your mind's eye, you increase the likelihood of it happening.

We may all look at things from different points of view, but everyone is capable of healing. It's a matter of perspective.

All addicts can be healed, but first they have to believe it.

11: PRACTICE MAKES PERFECT

I t doesn't take a brain surgeon to understand the brain.
Let's say that you want to copy a movie or some videos
and you open a pack of DVDs, all shiny and new.

Look at the laser side of a disc. Can you see anything there?
Not yet, as no data has been imprinted on it.

After burning the video, look at the laser side again. Notice
any changes? You should. There's now information on it, so a
faint change in appearance is visible.

Easy to understand, right?

Now you know how brains work. You don't have to be a
neuroscientist to comprehend basic neuroscience.

Perhaps there's *a bit* more to it, and grasping that simple
concept doesn't qualify you to operate on someone's brain, but
that is really all you need to know when it comes to chemical
balancing.

If we start at the beginning, babies are fairly similar to a fresh
new DVD. There's not much there, outside of instinctual wiring
such as reflexes (rooting, stepping, startle response, etc.) and
other 'preprogramming' such as sensory input processing, motor
control and language abilities. Despite coming in different
packages, babies just eat, sleep, cry, coo and poop.

But then they change and become different. Here's how it
happens neuroscientifically:

As discussed in Chapter 1, your brain features 100 billion
neurons — or little 'thinking' cells — with axons that are
oriented in the manner that 'you' direct them. It is as if you had
100 billion foot soldiers in your head, all marching to the

general's orders. Consciousness is first in command.

Your brain can also be likened unto a garden, with flowers and weeds both capable of growing there, pending the focus and habits of the gardener who tends it. Or if you prefer to be indoors, our brains are like computers. We are all born with the same basic hardware and software.

Not many people recognize that our brains are really about wiring, that portions of our brains are moving around … but those neurons are indeed wriggling and jiggling like the legs of the spider inside the *Old Lady Who Swallowed A Fly*.

In 1949, Canadian neuropsychologist Donald Hebb published a book entitled *The Organization of Behavior* in which he stated, "When an axon of cell A is near enough to excite cell B and repeatedly or persistently takes part in firing it, some growth process or metabolic change takes place in one or both cells such that A's efficiency, as one of the cells firing B, is increased."

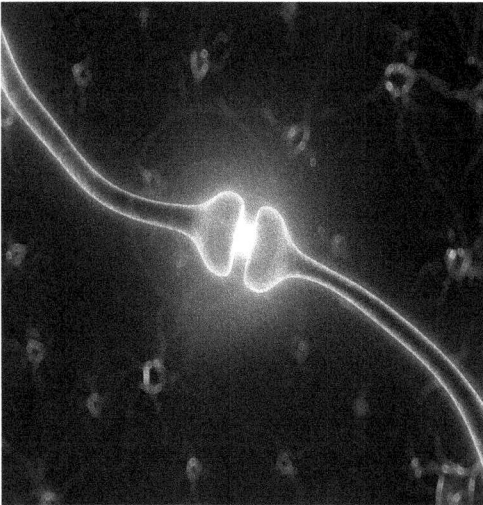

Translated, it means "neurons that fire together, wire together."

Neurons that fire together, wire together. Neurons that fire together, wire together. Neurons that fire together, wire together.

Now that you have read it a few times, the concept is wired together in your brain.

This is what is known as "Hebb's Law" and it may be the single most important piece of science to understand if you want to affect real change in your life.

Like a 100 billion-sided Rubik's Cube, there are nearly an infinite number of potential configurations for a human brain. The normal, six-sided Rubik's cube with nine squares per side has more than 43 quintillion possible configurations. Thanks to all of those wriggling and jiggling neurons, there are those who have calculated that the brain has more potential orientations than there are atoms in the universe.

That's a lot of variation!

As similar as babies are initially, they develop very uniquely as their minds begin to form while they experience different things. Whatever neurons of theirs that fire together will wire together, so as babies develop, their neurons create different patterns.

For example, what if one child is raised in Alaska and another in Ecuador? Chances are good that the former child's brain will develop the neural pattern for igloo much faster than the latter.

What if one child is born into an affluent family where both parents are mathematics professors while the other is born into poverty and never receives any formal schooling? Clearly, their brains will develop much differently.

If a child is neglected by his parents as a toddler, gets picked on in first grade, befriends a trouble-maker in sixth grade and then smokes marijuana as an eighth-grader, his brain will link all of those items together in a pattern. When he sees his mother and father guess what may happen? His brain connects the neural dots and he might feel like using some weed.

Neurons that fire together, wire together.

Conversely, if a child is treated well by his parents as a toddler, fits in well with the other kids in first grade and is popular in sixth grade what's the likelihood that he will smoke marijuana as an eighth grader? Probably less so. Will seeing his parents trigger a desire to use drugs. Probably not.

Those are greatly simplified scenarios, of course, but this is precisely how the brain develops. This is linked to that, which is linked to this and that … all coming together to form a neural network, what we experience as *an identity*. Each time a particular pattern is reinforced, the electrical-chemical link between neurons is strengthened. If a particular pattern is not reinforced, or not discovered in the first place, it either fades or doesn't ever show up at all.

Use it or lose it.

We all quickly diverge into these differing brain patterns. Over time, brain scans can pick this up. Unlike the scans of babies' brains, which are very similar, teen brain scans are wildly divergent.

Teens have begun to establish identities and yet are still figuring themselves out. They still have their futures filled with significant potential ahead of them, they can still think things such as "I want to be a professional baseball player" or "I want to join the military" or "I want to get married and have kids." They also think things like, "I can do this" or "I cannot do that" or "This is awesome" or "This is terrible" as well as "This is a hammer" and "This is an igloo."

All of those things are potential neural patterns for them.

During these years, some patterns get strengthened more than others. The strong ones appear on brain scans as thicker lines in denser regions, while patterns not attended to grow dimmer in sparsely lit regions. In neurochemistry, this is called pruning.

If a teen gives up on his dream of being president, the "I am going to be president" pathway fades, along with everything that would have been linked to that pathway. When one becomes hopeless, the hope pathway never lights up. If a teen focuses on "I can do this" then *that* neural pathway grows stronger and the "I cannot do this" pathway fades.

As Henry Ford said, "Whether you think you can or think you can't, you're right!"

Just as you trim a few branches off a tree so that the others grow stronger — pruning — the human brain does the same. If some neural pathways are pruned, the others grow stronger. Neural connections that are reinforced are retained, while those that aren't just fade to black.

Creatures of habit, all of us.

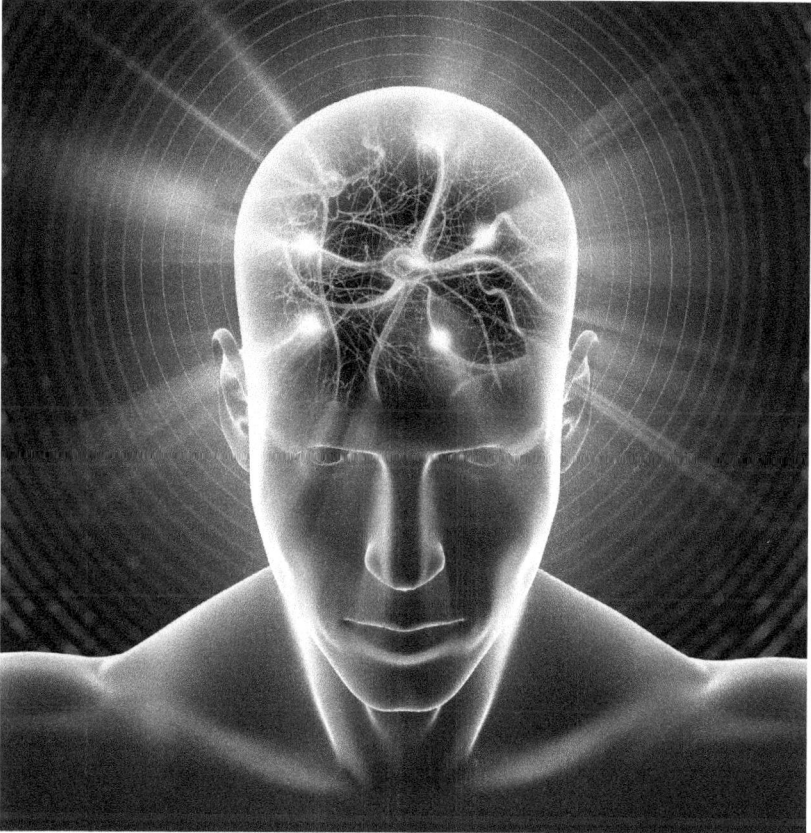

The brain works very similar to how rivers are formed. Sprinkle a few drops of water in a dry field, nothing happens. Keep pouring water, a stream will form over time. Continually add water and a river results, now capable of grabbing more rain because of its increased size.

How do you dry up that river? Stop adding water.

In the brain, if you sprinkle a few thoughts around, nothing happens. Keep practicing those thoughts, a neural pathway begins to form. Continually focus on those thoughts and the result is a strengthened pattern with which the thinker identifies.

How do you change a strengthened thought pattern, an identity that you don't like?

You change the way you think! It's as simple as that.

Changing the way you think can be difficult because of all the mind muscle you have developed by working out certain thoughts, whether it is "I like ice cream" or "I hate my boss."

If the river is mighty, it will be a challenge to divert its flow, but if you take a shovel and scoop a little dirt out of the riverbank, soon the water will go in a new direction.

Same with your thoughts. It's called neuroplasticity. The brain is not as hard and fixed as we once thought it to be, it is really more soft and flexible. It's not like steel, it's more like plastic. If someone wants to change their identity, they have to change their perception of themselves and of their circumstances.

When they do so in a healthy way, the brain balances.

One momentary idea isn't enough to counteract years of bad swing thoughts. Beliefs are thought patterns. If you practice worrying about hitting a bad golf shot, you become perfect at it. If you practice thinking about how bad your life is, you become depressed. But if you practice gratitude, you feel it.

Hebb's Law is how we got here and Hebb's Law is how we will get to where we want to go. We want to practice being hopeful, practice being forgiving, practice being drug-free, practice being happy.

Neurons that fire together, wire together.

Practice makes perfect.

12: THE VOLCANO

Human beings are a lot like volcanoes.

Most of the time they are peaceful, perhaps even beautiful, but every once in awhile they erupt and cause a lot of damage.

Suppose a volcano were about to erupt and several government officials determined it would be a good idea to cap it with a very large, heavy lid.

Would such an idea work? Maybe for a few hours. The lid would certainly trap the heat in and hold down the bubbling lava, at least temporarily.

Then what would happen? That's right, the pressure inside the volcano would build … and build … and build … until it exploded … blowing the lid off … and the lava would come pouring out after all.

That's pretty much how human beings, mental health issues and drugs interact, too.

The mountainous part of a volcano is like a human body, while the lava is negative emotion welling up inside. The lid is whatever drug or negative behavior is used in an attempt to contain those bad feelings, even to suppress them.

If a man is feeling anxious and depressed, he may use heroin to cover up that pain … or if a woman who is feeling intense anger, she may drink alcohol in an attempt to drown her rage … or a teenager may smoke marijuana to deal with stress and resentment … others do things like go on costly shopping sprees, obsess over their bodies, avoid social occasions or perform any number of potentially dysfunctional behaviors as a cover on a boiling pot of emotions.

In most cases, the emotional lava within each person is going to explode and end up creating a human being who is a hot mess, often seeking more or heavier lids (drugs) in an attempt to hold the lava back.

The 'put a lid on it' strategy never works, neither for volcanoes nor for human emotions.

The only guaranteed approach to making a volcano safe is dealing with the lava!

You cannot tame an active volcano with a cover, but you could make it permanently dormant if you found a way to cool the lava so it doesn't erupt and burn everything in its path … or perhaps find a way to eliminate the molten rock altogether.

Guess what? It's the same with the drug problem.

The most effective way to deal with this epidemic is not to find better or more powerful drugs to use, but to tame or reduce triggering emotions.

There are five primary feelings that most addicts relate to and nearly all of them acknowledge these as significant triggers: depression, anxiety, anger, boredom and physical pain. (A correlated reason for using is ignorance, but that's not a triggering emotion as much as it is a need for education.)

Virtually every reason for using drugs can be linked to one of those primary five feelings. Grief over the death of a loved one is similar to depression, using under peer pressure is a form of anxiety, partying with drugs because there is nothing better to do is a cousin of boredom, etc. (We keep it to these five because of simplicity and relatability, as most addicts will closely identify with one of those primary emotions, sometimes all five.) When we pay too much attention to the drugs being used, we neglect the underlying mental health issues involved.

If you remove the lid off a capped volcano, the lava is still going to be there as a threat. If you remove a drug from an addict, the underlying reason for using — hot emotions — will be laying in wait.

It's why addressing mental health issues is imperative, because negative emotion only strengthens the resolve of the hijacker. Depression, anxiety, anger, boredom and physical pain serve as ammunition for the attacker.

If we want to successfully combat addiction and mental health problems, we need to disarm the hijacker by dealing with the underlying causes of those issues.

We calm a volcano by effectively managing or transforming the lava. We win the drug war and heal mental health struggles through chemical balance.

13: THE GPS

Many automobiles and most cell phones these days come equipped with navigation capability. If you want to get directions to your destination, just fire up the global positioning satellite on whatever device you have in front of you and off you go.

As long as it is working correctly, you can rely upon a GPS to lead you to your destination. If you stop listening to its guidance, you can get lost. Would you ever ignore it if you needed assistance on what turn to take next? Of course not.

All human beings come equipped with such navigational systems.

We call them emotions.

Your emotions are the GPS for your observing mind, a feedback loop for chemical balancing. The primary clue in determining how close you are to achieving balance is how you feel. Generally speaking, if you are at peace, you are on a balanced path and heading in the right direction. If you aren't, you are off your path.

Simple examples make this most clear.

If you are in a burning building, you will feel fear, which motivates you to get out of the building. When you do so, your fear subsides, and you are again at peace.

If you are lonely because you don't have friends, that loneliness is a motivator to find friends. If that were your only issue, and you find friends, you will be at peace.

If you are nervous before a test, and that nervousness gets you to study so that you know the material, what happens when you know the material? Confidence replaces the anxiety and you are at peace.

If you are insecure because you worry too much about what other people think of you, the feeling of low self-esteem can be offset by learning how to focus only on oneself. Peace will soon follow.

Our emotions shift when our perspective shifts. It's mental evolution, followed by behavioral change.

Bottom line, whenever you feel a negative emotion, it is nudging you in a different direction, a motivator to get you to alter your perspective and get you back on the path toward chemical balance. Positive emotions operate as a reinforcer, a good indicator that you are headed the right way.

Many of us spend much of our lives hoping for external events to make us happier, but relying on things to always go your way is clearly a low-percentage strategy, whereas shifting your focus guarantees success.

Qualities such as perseverance, acceptance, gratitude and hope work in all situations. When you work on those virtues, your brain produces chemicals that balance your emotions.

What this means is that all emotions are actually good for you. Like the heat you feel from the top of a red-hot stove, emotions are warning signs to go in another direction. You can trust your emotions. They are teaching you something about what to do in your life.

It's why famed psychologist Carl Jung stated, "What you resist, persists."

When you refuse to learn from your emotions and do not deal with them, they continue and often get worse. Many people cover up their negative emotions by using drugs or respond to them with dysfunctional behaviors. Either option ultimately serves to make brain chemistry more imbalanced. It's like putting a cap on a volcano — eventually the pressure is going to build and it's going to explode.

Sometimes emotions can be deceiving in the short term (such as the relief someone feels after using certain drugs), but over the long haul emotions are a very reliable guide in balancing your brain.

Depression, anxiety and resentment are normal feelings, but that doesn't make them permanent. Emotional suffering only exists because of perception. All negative emotion can be reduced or removed by embracing it, which leads to a significant shift in perception.

Not many people are willing to be grateful for their troubles, but most everyone who succeeds at healing says the same thing: "It made me who I am today."

So trust your emotions. Let them be your tour guide through life. They will tell you where to go. If you take a wrong turn, they will let you know.

"Rerouting," says the GPS ... as well as the friendly inner voice inside your head and heart.

Your feelings aren't bad for you. Learn from them.

If you have hope, happiness is always just around the corner.

14: THE WATERFALL

Y ou can be in the same circumstances as another person … and yet completely different at the same time.
Like relativity, it all depends upon your point of view.

Imagine that you and a friend are kayaking in a river, headed toward a waterfall. Without thinking about it much, you might say that you are in the same situation.

But let's add a bit more to the equation.

Your friend is in her own kayak, a mile behind you, whereas you are 10 feet from the falls. She has a paddle and you don't. She is awake and you are asleep.

Same situation, yet drastically different!

While you are both facing potential danger, certainly you are in a far more treacherous position. If you do nothing, you are soon going over the falls. Even if you start paddling like crazy with your hands, it will probably be too late.

But your friend? As long as she paddles well before she reaches the danger zone, she will be just fine.

It's the difference between being proactive and reactive, and it makes all the difference in the world for someone dealing with addiction or healing from mental health issues.

Ups and downs are a natural part of life, they are practically unavoidable, though staying away from low lows like drug relapse or deep depression or panic attacks can be done if you remember one thing.

You must be proactive. You must paddle early.

If you wait, it's too late.

For anyone who is struggling, the way to safety is through paddling by using coping skills. (We will cover all of the best skills in Chapter 16.) You know you are doing well when you are at peace, which is chemical balance. On a river, peace is the calm, smooth water, while imbalance is the chaos of going over the falls.

Due to relativity, some people find themselves in better positions to succeed. If you woke up and your boat were still a half-mile upstream, you wouldn't need to panic … but if you were to find yourself on the edge of the falls, look out.

The goal of this book is to inspire hope and a clear pathway to healing —then it is up to each individual to begin paddling as early as possible. Do not wait until danger shows up. There are plenty of warning signs along the way to remind you to start paddling before the point of no return.

On a river, the current will start going faster and you can feel the kayak speeding up. The water will get choppier and you can start to see white caps, an indication of turbulence. People on the shore might scream at you, "Be careful! Danger ahead!"

It is the same with addiction and mental health. When you aren't feeling peaceful, life can seem as if it is racing by. Your emotions get choppier and you can see signs of turmoil, such as relationship and financial stressors, or perhaps your grades are falling. Family and friends might even scream at you, "Be careful! Danger ahead!"

These are all signs of the need to paddle your life in a new direction.

Sometimes, when people start to feel better, they stop doing

the things they need to do. Imagine paddling for just a few minutes on a kayak until you reach a calm area, then you take a nap. What happens next? You may start to drift.

Just as it is hard to paddle near the edge of the falls, it is hard to apply coping skills during intense drug cravings or during the depths of depression or the height of anxiety.

So don't take anything for granted. When you are feeling good, go with the flow. The most progress in life is often made when the stream is gentle … because then it is easier to row, row, row your boat.

15: THE BALANCING ACT

What's the opposite of tall? What's the opposite of fat? What's the opposite of black?

Did you say short, thin and white?

Wrong, wrong and wrong.

Scientist Niels Bohr spent most of his professional life studying atomic structure and quantum theory. As such, he knew a thing or two million about the makeup of the world we live in.

Albert Einstein said, "Look deep into nature and then you will understand everything better."

Bohr did just that, looking deep into nature and finding that opposites do not really exist. His family coat of arms included the Latin slogan, *"Contraria Sunt Complementa,"* which means opposites are complementary.

There really are no opposites in the physical world. Things are better understood as complements to each other, one definition of complementary being "mutually supplying each other's lack."

Short is a complement to tall, as shortness is really just a lack of tallness. Thin is a complement to fat, as thinness is really just a lack of fatness. White is a complement to black, as whiteness is really just a lack of blackness. And so on and so on.

We should think of the physical world in terms of its complementary nature, how most properties can be evaluated on a continuum and not as opposites. There isn't an opposite for 93 degrees Fahrenheit, but if you remove some heat by slowing the vibration of molecules, you have cold.

Similarly, light and dark are not opposites. Add a little light and darkness diminishes by a corresponding amount.

Bohr's coat of arms also included the ancient symbol for balance, the taijitu, better known as the yin yang. He was smitten with it because, indeed, the universe is all about balance.

There are dozens of fundamental physical constants (i.e. the speed of light, the Planck constant, the varying masses of electrons, protons and neutrons, etc.) that are so precise, were any of them to be slightly off, the universe as we know it might not exist. If the values of these constants were imbalanced, this would likely be a strangely different world, if there would be a world at all. For example, if the sun were closer to the earth we would burn out, or if it were farther away we would freeze.

Behaviorally, the need for balance is obvious.

We all know that exercise is good for you, and not exercising at all can be detrimental to your health. So does that mean working out 10 hours a day is good for you? Of course not. Not only can you over-exert yourself, becoming consumed with exercise can be an addiction that leads to dysfunction in other areas.

It's the same with nutrition, as we have all heard that we should "eat a balanced diet" many times in our lives. There is nothing wrong with an occasional donut, just don't make it a habit to gobble up a baker's dozen every day! And certainly it is possible to become too focused on calorie consumption that you don't eat enough, nor do you want to eat five heads of lettuce or drink three gallons of orange juice daily.

Really, it's like *Goldilocks and the Three Bears* … too hot, too cold, just right!

Most importantly, the human brain is also all about balance as well.

As noted in prior chapters, the 100 billion neurons in your head are each loaded with neurotransmitters that are

chemically comparable or even complementary to many street drugs and certain medicines.

To review (which is putting Hebb's Law into action), the reason why opiates such as heroin work is because the brain comes equipped with a natural counterpart called endorphins. Cocaine significantly increases the amount of dopamine in the brain, which is the reason for the high feeling associated with stimulant use. Sedatives such as alcohol and benzodiazepines imitate a neurochemical called GABA, while marijuana (anandamide) and even psychedelics (DMT) are believed to have natural mimics already in the brain.

Using street drugs or misusing prescription medicine typically throws natural brain chemistry out of balance, which leads to all sorts of dysfunction, including withdrawal symptoms and sometimes fatal overdose.

Similarly, mental health issues are also linked to brain chemistry. When one is low in serotonin production, the resulting feeling is called depression, which again is what the pharmaceutical industry labels a *chemical imbalance*. Low amounts of GABA have been linked to ADHD, hypertension and panic attacks.

In both addiction and mental health, restoring the brain to proper functioning is a balancing act, establishing harmony among those neurochemicals.

Thousands of years ago the renowned philosopher Aristotle recognized what Bohr later determined scientifically — that reality is loaded with complements (not opposites) varying by degree.

Regarding character traits, Aristotle described humans as possessing virtues that are either "deficient" or in "excess" until they reach the "virtuous mean," or the balance point between the two.

Courage is a virtuous mean. If one is deficient in courage, he is a coward. If one is excessive in courage, he is reckless.

Discipline is a virtuous mean. If one is deficient in discipline, she is indulgent. If one is excessive in discipline, she is obsessive.

Aristotle gave many more examples, including the virtuous mean of forgiveness (deficient is resentful, excessive is enabling) and humor (prudish, buffoonery).

You might be a coward if you are afraid to take any risks, but driving 110 mph down the highway doesn't make you courageous, it makes you reckless. If you cannot forgive someone, you may feel resentful toward them, but if you go too far in the other direction, you may open yourself up for further victimization. And if you can't take a joke you might be called a prude, but that does not mean you should be cracking jokes in front of a judge or at a funeral.

Bottom line, as human beings we demonstrate optimal character when we are balanced. This is what the yin yang is all about, the balancing of energies … and as Einstein revealed, *everything* is energy.

One of the most common interpretations of the taijitu symbol is the notion that yin (female) and yang (male) are two halves that ultimately make a complete whole inside each of us. The best way to think of this is that the balancing of feminine and masculine energies inside ourselves is the surest way to heal. We all benefit when we are compassionate, confident, forgiving, assertive, patient, courageous, nurturing, wise and hopeful.

That's how the brain is restored to balance.

You know you are out of balance when one of those qualities is deficient, because you can *feel* it. Impatience, for example, is an easy emotion to identify and a neurochemical nudge in the right healing direction of patience. Same with resentment, insecurity, cowardice, hopelessness and many more.

Let's say you are walking through the woods on a nice, clear path and you take a wrong turn, going deep into the forest and finding yourself lost in the dark. There you encounter a snake, a bear, or perhaps brush up against some poison ivy. What would the negative aspect of the above situation propel you to do? That's right, inspire you to go in another direction and head back to the peaceful path!

Similarly, if you are proceeding smoothly in life and then take a wrong turn, what happens? All sorts of chaos, such as emotional disturbance, marital discord, financial distress. What's the proper thing to do? Get back on the balanced path!

It's your own internal GPS at work, suggesting where to go.

If you are at peace, you are on the right path. If you aren't, try walking in a different direction.

16: THE MAP

I
f you want to follow a new path or want to walk beside someone who is trying to do so, it typically helps to have directions to follow.

You must still follow your own heart, but picking up the breadcrumbs along the trail that others have successfully walked can be a good strategy. While your own emotions are ultimately your ideal guide, they can be confusing … which is why having a picture painted for you can be helpful.

Like a perfect cake from a bakery, a healthy brain requires all the right ingredients in all the right amounts. When our neurotransmitters have the right chemistry, we feel peace in our heads and our hearts. As discussed in the relativity chapter, there are many different roads to get there, but the same basic methods lead most people toward wellness.

So here is a holistic map for healing — basically the answers to the test of life's balancing act — with simple mental, physical and spiritual suggestions pointing toward proven methods for producing the types of neurochemicals generally needed for fine-tuning the brain.

All of the suggested coping skills or activities listed below have been linked to the release of endorphins, dopamine, serotonin, oxytocin, GABA and other 'natural drugs' that we all can produce. (There are dozens of studies to support this treatment approach. See references on page 93.)

They are grouped into four categories, the first three being High Impact, Low Impact and H_2O Impact. In our experience,

High Impact skills tend to produce the greatest effects with the quickest results and are activities you can do by yourself. Low Impact skills are more passive, may not require as much effort and may require another person to be involved. As for H_2O Impact? Well, let's just say every neurochemical drop counts!

The final category is Spirituality, which is the home of hope … and the gold standard for recovery. A simple shift toward positive perception alters consciousness and produces wondrous healing effects on the mind and body.

Read through the list and see what interests you the most, or perhaps what is most suited to your relative situation. (The more the merrier, quite literally!) Then work with your family, friends, counselors, teachers or even through self-study to master these skills.

It is recommended that you work on one or two of the skills listed in the High and Low Impact categories while eventually addressing most, if not all, of the virtues in the Spirituality group.

Remember, practice makes perfect ... and perfection is chemical balance.

HIGH IMPACT
Exercise

Massive endorphin producer!

Exercise is nature's most merciful and forgiving activity,

because it eliminates so much of the 'bad energy' that we build up inside of ourselves while replacing it with 'good energy.'

Nearly every healthy neurochemical is affected by exercise, but working on physical fitness is basically akin to hitting the endorphin lottery. Anyone who is struggling with addiction or mental health issues should make it a high priority to add to their recovery repertoire.

Don't overdo it at first, of course, and consult with a physician if you have health concerns, but a casual 30-minute walk several times a week is a great start.

One well-studied form of exercise that does a wonderful job of balancing the brain in addition to the body is yoga. Martial arts, such as karate and taekwondo, are very beneficial as well.

Meditation

This is perhaps the most effective holistic exercise that man has ever practiced, improving the mind, body and spirit.

Many studies have demonstrated that meditation is a wonderful coping skill, stimulating the pituitary gland and hypothalamus to increase production of endorphins, serotonin, dopamine and GABA, while lowering stress-inducing cortisol levels in the bloodstream. It's the complete package.

There are many different types of meditation, but beginners can try guided meditations that are relatively simple and can easily be found online.

Music

Most everyone loves music, and the reason is energetic. It is a mood-altering vibration!

Classical music, in particular, does the body good. It has been shown to stimulate the release of serotonin, making it a natural antidepressant. Listening to music tends to decrease stress, while performing music releases endorphins and can provide the musician with a natural high.

Singing out loud to your favorite song, listening to soothing music and learning how to play a new instrument are all great coping skills.

Mindfulness

A state of higher awareness, mindfulness can lead to a constant state of peace that maintains brain balance.

It means staying in the present moment, not regretting the past nor worrying about the future. It's about focusing on *now*, including noticing thoughts and physical sensations in such a way that leads to emotional acceptance, not resistance.

It can be learned by anyone who simply wants to be mentally and physically healthier. There are many great mindfulness teachers and some very good mindfulness books and DVDs readily available on the internet.

Nutrition

It should go without saying how important a proper diet is to mental and physical health, but you don't have to just go green to balance your brain.

Working with a nutritionist is ideal, but as a jumpstart here are foods that have been shown to trigger 'good' neurochemicals.

- Chocolate releases endorphins and anandamide, which is the neurotransmitter that marijuana mimics in the brain. Dark chocolate is best.

- Spicy foods release endorphins, which means chili peppers and hot sauce at your favorite Mexican restaurant can be *good* for your mood!
- Foods high in protein (meat, turkey, fish) stimulate the release of endorphins, serotonin and dopamine.
- Carbohydrates such as pasta, bread and sugars are quick ways to boost serotonin … but consume in moderation, of course. (Food itself is an addiction for many people, so if that's the case for you, please look elsewhere on this list for the natural comfort that your brain can create. Food should not be the primary source of endorphin production, for example.)
- Needless to say, don't forget to eat your veggies!

Laughter

The expression "Laughter is the best medicine" is not just a cliche, it may be biologically correct!

Not only is a good giggling fit an obvious way to take your mind off stressful thoughts, it produces endorphins and serotonin through both psychological and physical effects.

It's why watching funny sitcoms or movies on a regular basis is a good idea. Always try to have a sense of humor about circumstances out of your control, if appropriate.

Relaxation

Chill out.

Seriously, just chill out. Take a break. Sit down and relax. Watch a cloud drift across the sky for three minutes. Do nothing at all!

Or take a long, warm bath. Hope is dope … and so is soap!

We are human beings not human doings. Relaxing helps reduce cortisol and can elevate GABA, inducing a sense of peace that helps balance the brain.

There are many different types of techniques, including progressive muscle relaxation, visualization and hypnosis.

Creativity

Doing anything you love tends to feel good, making creativity a vital part of brain balancing.

Studies have shown that the creative process produces endorphins. Elite artists and musicians and teachers and athletes and pretty much anyone in any activity generally find ways to express their craft in a unique way, and the resulting release of positive neurotransmitters is a significant payoff in that pursuit.

Even experiencing the creativity of others — such as going to a museum or attending a concert or reading a poem — also feels good for similar reasons.

Deep breathing

This one is a no-brainer for improving brain health.

Probably the most overlooked way to quickly enhance the quality of your life, regular deep breathing hits a neurochemical grand slam by releasing endorphins, GABA, dopamine and serotonin.

That means just by inhaling and exhaling in a certain way, consciously, you receive a little chemical cocktail of painkillers, sedatives and mood boosters.

Don't delay … start breathing right today. Practicing focused breathing for just three minutes twice a day is enough to begin training your brain to make it a habit.

Sleep

The word *endorphins* comes from the phrase "endogenous morphine," which means "morphine originating within the body."

Morphine is a powerful, highly addictive painkiller that is named after the Ancient Greek god Morpheus ... who was known as the god of sleep!

No surprise, then, that there is a high correlation between good sleep habits and endorphin production. Proper sleep also helps to regulate dopamine. In fact, much of the purpose of sleeping is its effectiveness in balancing brain chemistry.

It's a good idea to stick to a schedule that allows for at least seven hours of sleep per night, going to bed at around the same time (like 11 p.m.) every night. Don't watch TV in bed, all those high-def pixels are stimulating for the brain, and powering down that smartphone before laying down is a smart thing to do.

LOW IMPACT
Excitement

This one's quite simple and logical.

Excitement produces dopamine.

It's why addicts often report enjoying the chase for drugs, because of the excitement involved and anticipation of the high. That's dopamine.

You have heard of adrenaline junkies? Well, in addition to the stimulating hormone adrenaline, dopamine is typically released during thrill-seeking activities such as skydiving or race-car driving.

We are NOT suggesting that you go get fitted for a parachute or speed 110 mph down the highway! However, we are letting you know that anything that excites you will create a rush when, if repeated, it becomes a habit (thanks again, Mr. Hebb).

One significant component to recovery from addiction or mental health issues is to become excited about healing. Hope can inspire excitement, as you become secure in the knowledge that you can indeed feel better. Get psyched up for the chase for natural dope. Attending sporting events, going to amusement parks, exploring the wilderness, creating a new you … many new adventures can stimulate dopamine release.

Positive Thinking

As discussed during several earlier chapters, your mind is a very valuable thing! (That shouldn't come as a surprise.)

Practicing different ways of thinking can improve your outlook and worldview while creating different energy in the brain, which releases a wide variety of feel-good chemicals.

Cognitive Behavioral therapy (including Rational Emotive Behavior Therapy or REBT) can be especially effective, along with committing to simple philosophies such as "Don't Worry, Be Happy!" and "Fake It Until You Make It" and "That Which Doesn't Kill Me Makes Me Stronger" (or come up with your own mantra or life philosophy).

As Hebb's Law demonstrates, repeating positive affirmations and self-talk can bring about a healthier identity and greater self-esteem. Be optimistic. Practice, practice, practice!

Socializing

Many people tend to retreat into isolation when they are not feeling good, but engaging with good friends is a surefire way to boost one's mood.

Indeed, studies have shown that hanging out with your pals tends to be a better painkiller over time than painkillers.

Seeking friends is better for you than seeking drugs. And don't forget, hugs are free!

Studying

OK, maybe studying itself is not that fun, but turns out that learning is a significant brain reinforcer.

Experiments have demonstrated that learning things like a new language or developing math skills affects the reward pathway in the brain, which can mean increases in dopamine and endorphins as well as serotonin due to improved self-esteem.

So if you are in school, study. And if you are not, it's a good idea to learn something new every day. Understanding brain chemistry is a great jumpstart.

Sunlight

Don't hide inside all day long when you are feeling bad.

Get outside into the fresh air and soak up some sun; doing so has been demonstrated to produce vitamin D, which enhances serotonin production.

Once again, all things in moderation, please! Like Aristotle said and *The Story of the Three Bears* illustrated, stay away from excess and deficiency and experience what's "just right."

If you are cooped up in an office all day, try to eat lunch outside. Even a brief stroll in your neighborhood each day can be sufficient sunlight to help balance your brain.

Massage

Feels good and is good for you!

Acupuncture

Lots of little pins, lots more lovely endorphins!

Aromatherapy

Feeling stressed? The scent of vanilla has been shown to reduce anxiety. Feeling sad? The scent of lavender has been shown to reduce depression. Those and many more scents can enhance mood by affecting neurotransmitter production.

Pet Therapy

Puppies, kittens or whatever animal tickles your fancy also tickles your receptors.

Petting your pet produces endorphins and serotonin. Or go diving with dolphins, getting your animal action, sunlight, exercise and water all in one.

Smiling

Want a super quick way to produce endorphins, dopamine and serotonin? Flash those pearly whites! (Or metallic whites, or artificial whites, whatever the case may be.)

Believe it or not, even *faking* a smile when you don't feel like smiling 'tricks' the brain into thinking you are happier … and accordingly some happy brain juice is released. The brain is wired to release serotonin when your lips curl upward.

So smile more often, for no reason at all!

H₂O IMPACT
Drinking Water

Believe it or not, studies have shown that merely drinking water produces endorphins.

While obviously it is nothing like the effects of taking opioids, drinking water still releases a trickle of its chemical counterpart and proves the age-old adage that "every drop counts."

Perhaps you have heard that you should drink eight 8-ounce glasses of water a day? While that's a fine goal, it is generally more than enough for the average person.

A good rule of thumb is this: stay hydrated so that the feeling of thirst is rare. That means the more active you plan to be, the more water you need to remember to consume.

SPIRITUALITY

Focusing on enhancing non-physical aspects of oneself, such as developing virtues and finding meaning or purpose in your life, is an excellent way to bring the brain into better balance.

This does not mean that the Pope is Dope — we are not

talking about religion here. If religion works for you, that's fine.

But it has been scientifically demonstrated that certain personality characteristics are happiness highs, making you feel good naturally.

Virtues are free. Virtues are legal. Virtues boost the immune system, making you physically healthier as well as mentally. Virtues help relationships, not hurt them. Virtues are readily available to all of us.

Following is a list of virtues that are neurochemical gold mines for those in recovery or trying to improve their mental health:

Hope

It's quite literally dope, a significant endorphin producer.

Ask yourself this: When is the last time you felt hopeless and enjoyed feeling that way? That's right, never. Because hopelessness shuts down your endorphin system!

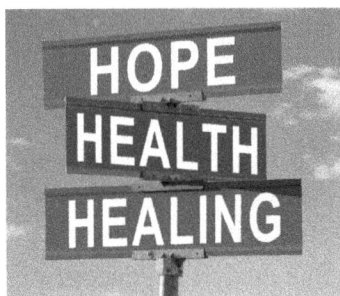

There is always reason for hope. Seek it every day. Expect positive outcomes. Watch inspiring movies. Read inspiring books. Practice being hopeful.

Healing comes when we balance our brains, which is possible no matter your age, gender, race, height, weight, sexual orientation, religious affiliation, hair color or any physical characteristic.

As long as you are trying to improve, there's always hope.

Compassion

Defined as a strong desire to alleviate the suffering of others, compassion has also been called a "helper's high." Why?

Endorphins, of course!

Practicing compassionate behavior is a fascinating paradox, because altruism is thought of as a selfless act, but it really benefits both parties. So hold the door open for others more often. Volunteer for a charity, or perform a random act of kindness, which has been shown to be more effective than antidepressants.

Like most everything, balance is key. You can suffer from compassion fatigue, so it is important to not extend too much energy in service to others while forgetting to take care of one's own needs.

Gratitude

You can probably guess by now what neurochemical feeling that being grateful produces.

(Hint: Rhymes with shmendorphins.)

Cultivating an attitude of gratitude is practically a requirement for long-term peace. Always look on the bright side. Create a list of things for which you are thankful. Reflect on what has gone well for you in your life. Surprise someone with a "Thank You" card, email or text.

Above all else, be grateful that you can heal yourself.

Courage

Any time you take a risk, such as skydiving or rescuing someone in danger, dopamine is involved.

Risk-taking requires courage, but that doesn't mean that your life has to be on the line. You can demonstrate courage by public speaking for the first time, by interviewing for your dream job, by riding a high-speed roller coaster, by joining a new club or sport, by going on a date, by getting married.

So be proactive. Face a fear. Embrace a new challenge or culture with an open mind.

You can even show "fake" courage and produce dopamine by watching scary movies or playing intense video games.

Forgiveness

Resentment puts a whole lot of stress on the body. Perhaps it's justifiable anger, but for certain harboring bitter feelings is harmful over the long haul.

Letting go, however, is precisely that. Letting go of negative energy. Forgiveness is about *not being energetically affected* by another person anymore, creating a more relaxed state of mind.

Forgiveness does not mean you have to bake a pie for your enemy. You do, however, have to change your mind. Simply writing a forgiveness letter and keeping it for yourself can help. But saying "I forgive you" to someone who has hurt you can be a powerful balancing experience as well.

Patience

Does traffic stress you out? Long lines at the store? Waiting for test results? Is there anything you can do about those circumstances to speed things up? Probably not.

Is there anything you can do about those circumstances to feel better? Certainly.

You can sedate your own mind and body by being patient. Practice it. Deliberately choose the *longest* line at the grocery store, it's a radical idea! While you are waiting, relax and breathe deeply. Or don't leave a movie theater until you have let everyone out before you. Be accepting and non-judgmental of yourself and others. GABA is your reward for a job well-done.

Don't always be in such a hurry. Patience is definitely a virtue, and a happy neurotransmitter to boot.

Plus, complaining all the time does *not* produce endorphins!

Integrity

Defined as a quality of being honest and fair, integrity certainly is a good mood booster. It sure beats trying to hide the truth and always whining with a shrill, "That's not fair!"

In fact, there was a study that equated a sense of fairness with higher levels of serotonin, so always thinking that you got a raw deal will clearly reduce happiness … just as unfairly taking advantage of others through deception eventually will.

Honesty is certainly one of the best policies, especially for your brain, as it reduces stress and provides a sense of integrity.

Passion

Whatever you are excited for and focused on produces dopamine.

When actively using, addicts increase their levels of dopamine merely when chasing after their drug of choice. No drug has actually been administered, yet they began feeling high beforehand simply because of the powerful effects of anticipation.

Well guess what happens when you are passionate about recovery? About self-improvement? About healing?

That's like injecting dopamine straight into your synapses.

Anyone with chemical dependence concerns should go after recovery with as much passion as they went after their drug of choice. You have to wake up thinking about endorphins and dopamine, you have to go to bed thinking of endorphins and dopamine and in between you think of endorphins and dopamine. Same with mental health. Neurotransmitters are the highest quality drugs available and you have a huge stash right there in your head.

Set specific and achievable goals. Celebrate when you accomplish them, no matter how small, like winning a board game or cleaning your bedroom (though that might be a BIG task for many of us). Behave like you did when you were a toddler, getting excited over every little thing, like playing with the box that your new toy came packaged in.

Use visualization techniques to increase dopamine production as well, seeing yourself succeeding at your goals … living a drug-free life … overcoming depression or anxiety … and fulfilling your long-term dreams.

As with the Butterfly Effect, a little passion will go a long way. Just a spark of interest or excitement in a new direction can eventually turn into a tornado of passion and healing.

Wisdom

Intelligence is when you are book smart. Wisdom is when you are spiritually smart.

Really, wisdom is understanding how to pull together all of the virtues … when and where to use them … and how to teach them to others.

Ignorance is not bliss, contrary to the old saying, but *wisdom is bliss*. American author F. Scott Fitzgerald said, "The test of a first-rate intelligence is the ability to hold two opposed ideas in mind at the same time and still retain the ability to function."

That's what wisdom allows you to do, reconciling otherwise difficult concepts in your own mind. It is a stress-reducer and endorphin-booster.

Wisdom allows you to understand cultural differences, comprehend relativity, tolerate diversity, relate to a variety of spiritual philosophies, effectively deal with adversity and remain graceful at all times. It is a mental and spiritual condition of peace.

Wisdom also allows for quick healings through insights and revelations, what are sometimes manifested in spontaneous remission. (This is a large emphasis of the book *New Eyes*, which is recommended for those ready to go deeper in the development of consciousness.)

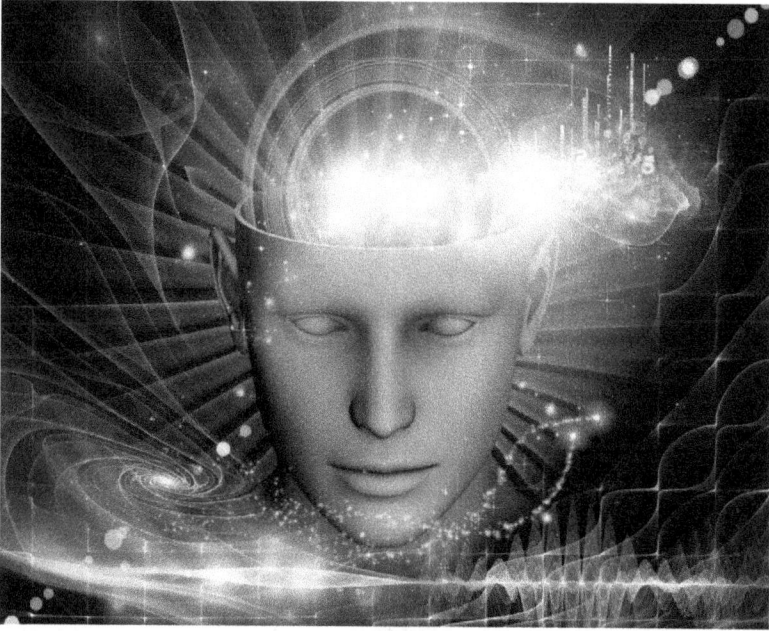

There was even a scientific study suggesting that in order to be wise one must have … wait for it … a balanced brain!

Love

It's hope, compassion, courage, forgiveness, patience, passion and wisdom all rolled into one.

When practiced by everyone who cares, it creates a *Safe Space* for healing. That concept is so important that we have dedicated the final chapter to this idea.

17: SAFE SPACE

T his may be the most important chapter in this book. It is written for the family members, friends, counselors, teachers, ministers and all other forms of helpers out there.

Everyone struggling with addiction or mental health issues needs you more than you know. They need you to believe in them. They need your hope.

A rising tide lifts all boats.

That is not just a pleasant expression, either, it's fact. It's true in the ocean and it's true with energy. As we learned in Chapter 9, *everything* is energy, and now we want to emphasize that *your* energy affects *their* energy.

In physics this is called entanglement, when two things are linked together in such a way that when one moves, so does the other ... simultaneously.

Imagine this: Wherever you are in the world reading this, if I were to raise my hand right now, is there any way you could know to also raise yours? Like, instantly? One would think not.

Except that's what happens in the lab with elementary particles that are energetically paired with each other. When one spins, the other does so at the exact same time, no matter how far apart they are.

According to conventional physics, there is no possible way a message or signal can be sent from one particle to the other without some passage of time, as travel even over a short amount of space has to take a nanosecond or two.

Albert Einstein called this, "Spooky action at a distance."

It is bizarre behavior, to say the least. Particles become linked, as there is an immediate, permanent connection between them. Whether it is 10 millimeters, 10 miles or 10 light years, particles are able to send information of some kind to each other immediately.

But you already knew this … if you've been to a sporting event … or to a wedding reception or hospital … or held a baby … or had a pet … you know, if you have been alive.

Energy connects us, instantaneously and permanently.

Here is how it works, simply stated:

1. Everything is made up of atoms.
2. Within those atoms are electrons.
3. Electrons absorb and release photons.
4. Photons are particles of light.
5. So atoms absorb and release light.
6. And you are entirely made up of atoms.
7. Which means *you* absorb and release light.

As you are made up of *a lot* of atoms, approximately a trillion times a trillion atoms, that means you absorb and release *a lot* of light. Since light is a form of electromagnetic energy, this means whenever people get connected with each other, they influence each other through entanglement. It's also known as *social contagion*.

Your energy is their energy.

Your hope is their hope.

Your endorphins, dopamine, serotonin and GABA can increase their endorphins, dopamine, serotonin and GABA.

We often call this *getting vibes* off of each other. When it is done in a supportive fashion with someone in need, it creates an enriching environment for them to grow.

A Safe Space. Between each other's hearts.

We can literally feel each other's feelings, making your viewpoint on someone who is struggling so very important.

Does a fussy baby calm down when comforted by an anxious person or a relaxed person? The answer is obvious. It's the same with addiction and mental health.

If someone is trying to recover from drug use and they feel your judgment and disappointment, they experience a negative energy that typically increases their desire to use in order to medicate that unpleasant emotional state. They often already feel shame and guilt — it doesn't help when they feel more negative vibes dumped on top of them.

It's also why hopelessness or pity for someone else is not an effective approach.

The best way to help someone in recovery is by *believing* that they can succeed ... by being patient ... by offering encouragement ... by inspiring them to believe in themselves.

If someone you care about is stranded on the other side of a river, don't just scream at them to swim over to where you are ... take the plunge yourself and swim over to them, put your arm around them, see the world through their eyes and then help them cross over to the safer, healthier side.

Joining a struggling friend *exactly where they are* is pivotal to progress. Don't assume they know what you know, nor expect them to be able to succeed right away. Mistakes happen, but we can grow from them. Don't shame someone for relapsing, ask them what they learned from the experience.

Energy entanglement demonstrates the power of compassion, as two or more people bond in a heartfelt way that facilitates a healthy emotional connection.

Fear, for sure, does not work well. Ask any parent if worrying about their depressed child helps much and ask any addict if the threat of punishment is sufficient to sustain a long-term recovery. They will say no. Negative energy breeds negative outcomes. But if you take the time to understand the message of this treatment approach, you can be a positive influence and more effective teacher.

Role models are not fearful, they send out good vibrations. Strong leaders do not waver, they stay confident. They inspire. They have hope.

They create Safe Spaces for healing.

Taken to the deepest level, it's called love. It's an all-encompassing, transformational energy.

Just as all the colors of a rainbow are rolled into one brilliant clear light, love combines all the virtues into one emotion. When you are in a Safe Space with another person, love elevates both of you. It's how we all heal.

Diverse people, united in hope.

REFERENCES

INTRODUCTION

Associated Press. (2010, May 13). AP IMPACT: After 40 years, $1 trillion, US War on Drugs has failed to meet any of its goals. Fox News. Retrieved from http://www.foxnews.com/world/2010/05/13/ap-impact-years-trillion-war-drugs-failed-meet-goals.html

Benedetti F., Mayberg H. S., Wager T. D., Stohler C. S., Zubieta J. K. Neurobiological mechanisms of the placebo effect. *Journal of Neuroscience* 25: 10390–10402, 2005. doi:10.1111/j.1749-6632.2009.04424.x

Center for Behavioral Health Statistics and Quality. (2015). Behavioral health trends in the United States: Results from the 2014 National Survey on Drug Use and Health (HHS Publication No. SMA 15-4927, NSDUH Series H-50). Retrieved from http://www.samhsa.gov/data/sites/default/files/NSDUH-FRR1-2014/NSDUH-FRR1-2014.htm#idtextanchor074

Groopman, J. (2004). *The Anatomy of Hope: How People Prevail in the Face of Illness.* United States: Random House Publishing Group.

National Alliance on Mental Illness. (2017). *Depression.* Retrieved from http://www.nami.org/Learn-More/Mental-Health-Conditions/Depression

National Center on Addiction and Substance Abuse at Columbia University. (2009). Shoveling Up II: The Impact of Substance Abuse on Federal, State and Local Budgets. New York, NY: The National Center on Addiction and Substance Abuse at Columbia University. Retrieved from http://www.centeronaddiction.org/addiction-research/reports/shoveling-ii-impact-substance-abuse-federal-state-and-local-budgets

Petrovic, P., Kalso, E., Petersson, K., & Ingvar, M. (2002). Placebo and Opioid Analgesia - imaging a shared neuronal network. *Science, 295*(5560), 1737-1740. doi:10.1126/science.1067176

Truven Health Analytics Inc. (2016). *Naltrexone (oral route).* Retrieved from http://www.mayoclinic.org/drugs-supplements/naltrexone-oral-route/side-effects/drg-20068408

CHAPTER 1

Lodish H., Berk A., Zipursky S. L., et al. (2000). Section 21.1, Overview of neuron structure and function. In *Molecular cell biology* (4th ed.). New York, NY: W. H. Freeman. Available from http://www.ncbi.nlm.nih.gov/books/NBK21535/

National Institute on Drug Abuse. (2007). Impacts of drugs on neurotransmission. Retrieved from https://www.drugabuse.gov/news-events/nida-notes/2007/10/impacts-drugs-neurotransmission

National Institute of Mental Health. (2016). *Brain Basics.* Retrieved from http://www.nimh.nih.gov/brainbasics/index.html

CHAPTER 2

Adinoff, B. (2004). Neurobiologic processes in drug reward and addiction. *Harvard Review of Psychiatry, 12*(6), 305–320. doi:10.1080/10673220490910844

Chao, J., & Nestler, E. J. (2004). Molecular neurobiology of drug addiction. *Annual Review of Medicine, 55*(1), 113–132. doi:10.1146/annurev.med.55.091902.103730

Dumas, E. O., & Pollack, G. M. (2008). Opioid tolerance development: A pharmacokinetic/pharmacodynamic perspective. *The AAPS Journal, 10*(4), 537–551. doi:10.1208/s12248-008-9056-1

DuPen, A., Shen, D., & Ersek, M. (2007). Mechanisms of opioid-induced tolerance and hyperalgesia. *Pain Management Nursing, 8*(3), 113–121. doi:10.1016/j.pmn.2007.02.004

Feng, Y., He, X., Yang, Y., Chao, D., H. Lazarus, L., & Xia, Y. (2012). Current research on opioid receptor function. *Current Drug Targets, 13*(2), 230–246. doi:10.2174/138945012799201612

Koob, G. F. (1997). Drug abuse: Hedonic homeostatic dysregulation. *Science, 278*(5335), 52–58. doi:10.1126/science.278.5335.52

Koob, G. F., & Volkow, N. D. (2010). Neurocircuitry of addiction. *Neuropsychopharmacology, 35*(4), 1051–1051. doi:10.1038/npp.2010.4

Munro, M. (2015). The hijacked brain. *Nature, 522*(7557), S46–S47. doi:10.1038/522s46a

National Institute on Drug Abuse. (2007). Impacts of drugs on neurotransmission. Retrieved from https://www.drugabuse.gov/news-events/nida-notes/2007/10/impacts-drugs-neurotransmission

Pierce, R. C., & Kumaresan, V. (2006). The mesolimbic dopamine system: The final common pathway for the reinforcing effect of drugs of abuse? *Neuroscience & Biobehavioral Reviews, 30*(2), 215–238. doi:10.1016/j.neubiorev.2005.04.016

CHAPTER 3

Bloomfield, M. A. P., Morgan, C. J. A., Egerton, A., Kapur, S., Curran, H. V., & Howes, O. D. (2014). Dopaminergic function in cannabis users and its relationship to cannabis-induced psychotic symptoms. *Biological Psychiatry, 75*(6), 470–478. doi:10.1016/j.biopsych.2013.05.02

Cryan, J. F., & Kaupmann, K. (2005). Don't worry "B" happy!: A role for GABA$_B$ receptors in anxiety and depression. *Trends in Pharmacological Sciences, 26*(1), 36–43. doi:10.1016/j.tips.2004.11.004

Farquhar-Smith, W. P., Egertová, M., Bradbury, E. J., McMahon, S. B., Rice, A. S. C., & Elphick, M. R. (2000). Cannabinoid CB1 receptor expression in rat spinal cord. *Molecular and Cellular Neuroscience, 15*(6), 510–521. doi:10.1006/mcne.2000.0844

Filbey, F. M., Aslan, S., Calhoun, V. D., Spence, J. S., Damaraju, E., Caprihan, A., & Segall, J. (2014). Long-term effects of marijuana use on the brain. *Proceedings of the National Academy of Sciences, 111*(47), 16913–16918. doi:10.1073/pnas.1415297111

Hoebel, B. G., Rada, P. V., Mark, G. P., & Pothos, E. (1999). Neural systems for reinforcement and inhibition of behavior: Relevance to eating, addiction, and depression. In D. Kahneman, E. Diener, & N. Schwarz (Eds.), *Well-being: Foundations of hedonic psychology* (pp. 558-572). New York, NY: Russell Sage Foundation.

National Institute on Drug Abuse. (2007). Impacts of drugs on neurotransmission. Retrieved from https://www.drugabuse.gov/news-events/nida-notes/2007/10/impacts-drugs-neurotransmission

Nikolaus, S., Antke, C., Beu, M., & Müller, H.W. (2010). Cortical GABA, striatal dopamine and midbrain serotonin as the key players in compulsive and anxiety disorders - results from in vivo imaging studies. *Reviews in the Neurosciences, 21*(2), 119-139. doi:10.1515/revneuro.2010.21.2.119

Strakowski, S. M., DelBello, M. P., & Adler, C. M. (2004). The functional neuroanatomy of bipolar disorder: A review of neuroimaging findings. *Molecular Psychiatry, 10*(1), 105–116. doi:10.1038/sj.mp.4001585

Torrey, E. F., Barci, B. M., Webster, M. J., Bartko, J. J., Meador-Woodruff, J. H., & Knable, M. B. (2005). Neurochemical markers for schizophrenia, bipolar disorder, and major depression in postmortem brains. *Biological Psychiatry, 57*(3), 252–260. doi:10.1016/j.biopsych.2004.10.019

University of Pennsylvania Health System. (2003). Stairway to recovery: The neurotransmitters that mediate addiction and mental illness. Retrieved from http://www.uphs.upenn.edu/addiction/berman/relapse/

van Hell, H. H., Vink, M., Ossewaarde, L., Jager, G., Kahn, R. S., & Ramsey, N. F. (2010). Chronic effects of cannabis use on the human reward system: An fMRI study. *European Neuropsychopharmacology, 20*(3), 153–163. doi:10.1016/j.euroneuro.2009.11.010

Young, S. N. (2007). How to increase serotonin in the human brain without drugs. *Journal of Psychiatry & Neuroscience : JPN, 32*(6), 394–399.

CHAPTER 4

Koob, G. F. (1997). Drug abuse: Hedonic homeostatic dysregulation. *Science, 278*(5335), 52–58. doi:10.1126/science.278.5335.52

Koob, G. F., & Le Moal, M. (2008). Addiction and the brain antireward system. *Annual Review of Psychology, 59*(1), 29–53. doi:10.1146/annurev.psych.59.103006.093548

Sangkuhl, K., Klein, T. E., & Altman, R. B. (2009). Selective serotonin reuptake inhibitors pathway. *Pharmacogenetics and Genomics, 19*(11), 907–909. doi:10.1097/fpc.0b013e32833132cb

Volkow, N. D., Chang, L., Wang, G.-J., Fowler, J. S., Franceschi, D., Sedler, M., ... Logan, J. (2001). Loss of dopamine transporters in methamphetamine abusers recovers with protracted abstinence. *The Journal of Neuroscience, 21*(23), 9414–9418. Retrieved from http://www.jneurosci.org/content/21/23/9414.full

CHAPTER 5

National Institute on Drug Abuse. (2012). Evidence-based approaches to drug addiction treatment: Pharmacotherapies. In *Principles of Drug Addiction Treatment: A Research-Based Guide* (3rd Ed.) (NIH Publication No. 12–4180). Retrieved from https://www.drugabuse.gov/publications/principles-drug-addiction-treatment-research-based-guide-third-edition/evidence-based-approaches-to-drug-addiction-treatment/pharmacotherapies

National Institute on Drug Abuse. (2014). CNS depressants: How do CNS depressants affect the brain and body? In *Research report series: Prescription drug abuse* (NIH Publication Number 15-4881). Retrieved from

National Institute on Drug Abuse. (2016). DrugFacts: Treatment approaches for drug addiction. Retrieved from https://www.drugabuse.gov/publications/drugfacts/treatment-approaches-drug-addiction

Torrens, M., Fonseca, F., Mateu, G., & Farré, M. (2005). Efficacy of antidepressants in substance use disorders with and without comorbid depression. *Drug and Alcohol Dependence, 78*(1), 1–22. doi:10.1016/j.drugalcdep.2004.09.004

CHAPTER 10

National Institute on Drug Abuse. (2012). Frequently asked questions: How effective is drug addiction treatment? In *Principles of Drug Addiction Treatment: A Research-Based Guide* (3rd Ed.) (NIH Publication No. 12–4180). Retrieved from https://www.drugabuse.gov/publications/principles-drug-addiction-treatment-research-based-guide-third-edition/frequently-asked-questions/how-effective-drug-addiction-treatment

CHAPTER 11

Hebb, D. O. O. (2002). *The organization of behavior: A neuropsychological theory* (New Ed.). Mahwah, NJ: Lawrence Erhlbaum Associates, Inc. (Original work published 1949).

CHAPTER 15

Edden, R. A. E., Crocetti, D., Zhu, H., Gilbert, D. L., & Mostofsky, S. H. (2012). Reduced GABA concentration in attention-deficit/Hyperactivity disorder. *Archives of General Psychiatry, 69*(7): 750-753. doi:10.1001/archgenpsychiatry.2011.2280

Shimada, M., Hasegawa, T., Nishimura, C., Kan, H., Kanno, T., Nakamura, T., & Matsubayashi, T. (2009). Anti-Hypertensive effect of γ-aminobutyric acid

(GABA)-rich Chlorella on high-normal blood pressure and borderline hypertension in placebo-controlled double blind study. *Clinical and Experimental Hypertension, 31*(4), 342–354. doi:10.1080/10641960902977908

Gauthier, I., & Nuss, P. (2015). Anxiety disorders and GABA neurotransmission: A disturbance of modulation. *Neuropsychiatric Disease and Treatment, 11*, 165-175. doi:10.2147/ndt.s58841

CHAPTER 16
Exercise

American Psychological Association, Dishman, R. K., & Sothmann, M. (2016). *Exercise fuels the brain's stress buffers.* Retrieved from http://www.apa.org/helpcenter/exercise-stress.aspx

Brown, R. A., Abrantes, A. M., Read, J. P., Marcus, B. H., Jakicic, J., Strong, D. R., ... Gordon, A. A. (2008). Aerobic exercise for alcohol recovery: Rationale, program description, and preliminary findings. *Behavior Modification, 33*(2), 220–249. doi:10.1177/0145445508329112

Fox, K. R. (1999). The influence of physical activity on mental well-being. *Public Health Nutrition,2*(3a): 411-418. doi:10.1017/s1368980099000567

Kim, Y. J., Cha, E. J., Kim, S. M., Kang, K. D., & Han, D. H. (2015). The effects of Taekwondo training on brain Connectivity and body intelligence. *Psychiatry Investigation, 12*(3), 335. doi:10.4306/pi.2015.12.3.335

Kinser, P. A., Goehler, L. E., & Taylor, A. G. (2012). How might yoga help depression? A neurobiological perspective. *EXPLORE: The Journal of Science and Healing, 8*(2), 118–126. doi:10.1016/j.explore.2011.12.005

Krishnakumar, D., Hamblin, M. R., & Lakshmanan, S. (2015). Meditation and yoga can modulate brain mechanisms that affect behavior and anxiety-A modern scientific perspective. *Ancient Science, 2*(1), 13–19. doi:10.14259/as.v2i1.171

Lakes, K. D., Bryars, T., Sirisinahal, S., Salim, N., Arastoo, S., Emmerson, N., ... Kang, C. J. (2013). The healthy for life Taekwondo pilot study: A preliminary evaluation of effects on executive function and BMI, feasibility, and acceptability. *Mental Health and Physical Activity, 6*(3), 181–188. doi:10.1016/j.mhpa.2013.07.002

Maddock, R. J., Casazza, G. A., Fernandez, D. H., & Maddock, M. I. (2016). Acute modulation of cortical glutamate and GABA content by physical activity. *Journal of Neuroscience, 36*(8), 2449–2457. doi:10.1523/jneurosci.3455-15.2016

National Institute on Drug Abuse. (2012). Frequently asked questions: Can exercise play a role in the treatment process? In *Principles of Drug Addiction Treatment: A Research-Based Guide* (3rd Ed.) (NIH Publication No. 12–4180). Retrieved from https://www.drugabuse.gov/publications/principles-drug-addiction-treatment-research-based-guide-third-edition/frequently-asked-questions/can-exercise-play-role-in-treatment-process

National Institute on Drug Abuse. (2012). Physical activity reduces return to cocaine seeking in animal tests. Retrieved from https://www.drugabuse.gov/news-events/nida-notes/2012/04/physical-activity-reduces-return-to-cocaine-seeking-in-animal-tests

Streeter C. C., Jensen J. E., Perlmutter R. M., et al. (2007). Yoga Asana sessions increase brain GABA levels: a pilot study. *Journal of Alternative & Complementary Medicine 13*(4), 419–426. doi:10.1089/acm.2007.6338

Streeter C. C., Whitfield T. H., Owen L., et al. (2010). Effects of yoga versus walking on mood, anxiety, and brain GABA levels: a randomized controlled MRS study. *Journal of Alternative & Complementary Medicine, 16*(11), 1145–1152. doi:10.1089/acm.2010.0007

Wang, J. (2013). Effects of exercise on stress-induced changes of Norepinephrine and serotonin in rat Hippocampus. *The Chinese Journal of Physiology, 56*(5), 245–252. doi:10.4077/cjp.2013.bab097

Meditation

Krishnakumar, D., Hamblin, M. R., & Lakshmanan, S. (2015). Meditation and yoga can modulate brain mechanisms that affect behavior and anxiety-A modern scientific perspective. *Ancient Science, 2*(1), 13–19. doi:10.14259/as.v2i1.171

Newberg, A. B., & Iversen, J. (2003). The neural basis of the complex mental task of meditation: Neurotransmitter and neurochemical considerations. *Medical Hypotheses, 61*(2), 282–291. doi:10.1016/s0306-9877(03)00175-0

Pace, T. W. W., Negi, L. T., Sivilli, T. I., Issa, M. J., Cole, S. P., Adame, D. D., & Raison, C. L. (2010). Innate immune, neuroendocrine and behavioral responses to psychosocial stress do not predict subsequent compassion meditation practice time. *Psychoneuroendocrinology, 35*(2), 310–315. doi:10.1016/j.psyneuen.2009.06.008

Rosenkranz, M. A., Lutz, A., Perlman, D. M., Bachhuber, D. R. W., Schuyler, B. S., MacCoon, D. G., & Davidson, R. J. (2016). Reduced stress and inflammatory responsiveness in experienced meditators compared to a matched healthy control group. *Psychoneuroendocrinology, 68,* 117–125. doi:10.1016/j.psyneuen.2016.02.013

Rubia, K. (2009). The neurobiology of meditation and its clinical effectiveness in psychiatric disorders. *Biological Psychology, 82*(1), 1–11. doi:10.1016/j.biopsycho.2009.04.003

Music

Dunbar, R. I. M., Kaskatis, K., MacDonald, I., & Barra, V. (2012). Performance of music elevates pain threshold and positive affect: Implications for the evolutionary function of music. *Evolutionary Psychology, 10*(4), 688-702. doi:10.1177/147470491201000403

Evers, S., & Suhr, B. (2000). Changes of the neurotransmitter serotonin but not of hormones during short time music perception. *European Archives of Psychiatry and Clinical Neuroscience, 250*(3), 144–147. doi:10.1007/s004060070031

MacDonald, R. A. R. (2013). Music, health, and well-being: A review. *International Journal of Qualitative Studies on Health and Well-Being, 8.* doi:10.3402/qhw.v8i0.20635

Salimpoor, V. N., Benovoy, M., Larcher, K., Dagher, A., & Zatorre, R. J. (2011). Anatomically distinct dopamine release during anticipation and experience of peak emotion to music. *Nature Neuroscience, 14*(2), 257–262. doi:10.1038/nn.2726

Thoma, M. V., La Marca, R., Brönnimann, R., Finkel, L., Ehlert, U., & Nater, U. M. (2013). The effect of music on the human stress response. *PLoS ONE, 8*(8), e70156. doi:10.1371/journal.pone.0070156

Mindfulness

Brewer, J. A., Bowen, S., Smith, J. T., Marlatt, G. A., & Potenza, M. N. (2010). Mindfulness-based treatments for co-occurring depression and substance use disorders: What can we learn from the brain? *Addiction, 105*(10), 1698–1706. doi:10.1111/j.1360-0443.2009.02890.x

Carlson, L. E., Speca, M., Patel, K. D., & Goodey, E. (2004). Mindfulness-based stress reduction in relation to quality of life, mood, symptoms of stress and levels of cortisol, dehydroepiandrosterone sulfate (DHEAS) and melatonin in breast and prostate cancer outpatients.*Psychoneuroendocrinology, 29*(4), 448–474. doi:10.1016/s0306-4530(03)00054-4

Hölzel, B. K., Carmody, J., Vangel, M., Congleton, C., Yerramsetti, S. M., Gard, T., & Lazar, S. W. (2011). Mindfulness practice leads to increases in regional brain gray matter density. *Psychiatry Research, 191*(1), 36–43. doi:10.1016/j.pscychresns.2010.08.006

Jacobs, T. L., Shaver, P. R., Epel, E. S., Zanesco, A. P., Aichele, S. R., Bridwell, D. A., ... Saron, C. D. (2013). Self-reported mindfulness and cortisol during a Shamatha meditation retreat. *Health Psychology, 32*(10), 1104–1109. doi:10.1037/a0031362

Matousek, R. H., Dobkin, P. L., & Pruessner, J. (2010). Cortisol as a marker for improvement in mindfulness-based stress reduction. *Complementary Therapies in Clinical Practice, 16*(1), 13–19. doi:10.1016/j.ctcp.2009.06.004

Taren, A. A., Gianaros, P. J., Greco, C. M., Lindsay, E. K., Fairgrieve, A., Brown, K. W., ... Creswell, J. D. (2015). Mindfulness meditation training alters stress-related amygdala resting state functional connectivity: A randomized controlled trial. *Social Cognitive and Affective Neuroscience, 10*(12), 1758–1768. doi:10.1093/scan/nsv066

Nutrition

Bendetti, F., Arduino, C., & Amanzio, M. (1999). Somatotopic Activation of Opioid Systems by Target-Directed Expectations of Analgesia. *The Journal of Neuroscience, 19*(9), 3639–364. Retrieved from http://www.jneurosci.org/content/19/9/3639.full

Dum, J. (1983). Activation of hypothalamic β-endorphin pools by reward induced by highly palatable food. *Pharmacology Biochemistry and Behavior, 18*(3), 443–447. doi:10.1016/0091-3057(83)90467-7

Fernstrom, J. D., & Wurtman, R. J. (1971). Brain serotonin content: Increase following ingestion of carbohydrate diet. *Science, 174*(4013), 1023–1025. doi:10.1126/science.174.4013.1023

Nehlig, A. (2013). The neuroprotective effects of cocoa flavanol and its influence on cognitive performance. *British Journal of Clinical Pharmacology, 75*(3), 716–727. doi:10.1111/j.1365-2125.2012.04378.x

Wurtman, R. J., Wurtman, J. J., Regan, M. M., McDermott, J. M., Tsay, R. H., & Breu, J. J. (2003). Effects of normal meals rich in carbohydrates or proteins on plasma tryptophan and tyrosine ratios. *American Journal of Clinical Nutrition, 77*(1), 128–132. Retrieved from http://ajcn.nutrition.org/content/77/1/128.full.pdf+html

Laughter

Berk, L. S., Tan, S. A., Fry, W. F., Napier, B. J., Lee, J. W., Hubbard, R. W., et al. (1989). Neuroendocrine and stress hormone changes during mirthful laughter. *American Journal of the Medical Sciences, 298,* 390–396. doi:10.1097/00000441-198912000-00006

Black, S., & Friedman, M. (1968). Effects of emotion and pain on adrenocortical function investigated by hypnosis. *British Medical Journal, 1*(5590), 477–481. doi:10.1136/bmj.1.5590.477

Codispoti, M., Gerra, G., Montebarocci, O., Zaimovic, A., Raggi, M. A., & Baldaro, B. (2003). Emotional perception and neuroendocrine changes. *Psychophysiology, 40*(6), 863–868. doi:10.1111/1469-8986.00104

Dunbar, R. I. M., Baron, R., Frangou, A., Pearce, E., van Leeuwen, E. J. C., Stow, J., ... van Vugt, M. (2011). Social laughter is correlated with an elevated pain threshold. *Proceedings of the Royal Society B: Biological Sciences, 279*(1731), 1161–1167. doi:10.1098/rspb.2011.1373

Mobbs, D., Greicius, M. D., Abdel-Azim, E., Menon, V., & Reiss, A. L. (2003). Humor Modulates the Mesolimbic reward centers. *Neuron, 40*(5), 1041–1048. doi:10.1016/s0896-6273(03)00751-7

Wilkins, J., & Eisenbraun, A. J. (2009). Humor theories and the physiological benefits of laughter. *Holistic Nursing Practice, 23*(6), 349–354. doi:10.1097/hnp.0b013e3181bf37ad

Zachariae, R., Bjerring, P., Zachariae, C., Arendt-Nielsen, L., Nielsen, T., Eldrup, E., et al. (1991). Monocyte chemotactic activity in sera after hypnotically induced emotional states. *Scandanavian Journal of Immunology, 34*(1), 71–79. doi:10.1111/j.1365-3083.1991.tb01522.x

Relaxation

Esch, T., & Stefano, G. B. (2010). The neurobiology of stress management. *Neuroendocrinology Letters, 31*(1), 19–39. Retrieved from https://www.researchgate.net/publication/255685315_The_neurobiology_of_s

tress_management

Taren, A. A., Gianaros, P. J., Greco, C. M., Lindsay, E. K., Fairgrieve, A., Brown, K. W., ... Creswell, J. D. (2015). Mindfulness meditation training alters stress-related amygdala resting state functional connectivity: A randomized controlled trial. *Social Cognitive and Affective Neuroscience, 10*(12), 1758–1768. doi:10.1093/scan/nsv066

Creativity

Baikie, K. A. (2005). Emotional and physical health benefits of expressive writing. *Advances in Psychiatric Treatment, 11*(5), 338–346. doi:10.1192/apt.11.5.338

Boso, M., Politi, P., Barale, F., and Enzo, E. (2006). Neurophysiology and neurobiology of the musical experience. *Functional Neurology, 21* (4), 187–191. Retrv from http://www.functionalneurology.com/index.php?PAGE=articolo_dett&ID_ISSU E=198&id_article=1885

Lane, M. R. (2005). Creativity and spirituality in nursing. *Holistic Nursing Practice, 19*(3), 122–125. doi:10.1097/00004650-200505000-00008

Monti, D. A., Peterson, C., Kunkel, E. J. S., Hauck, W. W., Pequignot, E., Rhodes, L., & Brainard, G. C. (2006). A randomized, controlled trial of mindfulness-based art therapy (MBAT) for women with cancer. *Psycho-Oncology, 15*(5), 363–373. doi:10.1002/pon.988

Deep Breathing

Kulkarni, D. D., & Bera, T. K. (2009). Yogic exercises and health – A psycho-neuro immunological approach. *Indian journal of physiology and pharmacology, 53*(1), 3–15. Retrieved from http://www.ijpp.com/IJPP%20archives/2009_53_1_Jan%20-%20Mar/3-15.pdf

Siswantoyo Y., & Aman, M. S. (2014). The effects of breathing exercise toward IgG, beta endorphin and blood glucose secretion. *Asia Pacific Journal of Education, Arts and Sciences, 1*(4), 27–32. Retrieved from http://apjeas.apjmr.com/wp-content/uploads/2014/09/APJEAS-2014-1-058.pdf

Sleep

Fox, K. R. (1999). The influence of physical activity on mental well-being. *Public Health Nutrition,2*(3a): 411-418. doi:10.1017/s1368980099000567

Volkow, N. D., Tomasi D., Wang G. J., Telang F., Fowler J. S., Logan J., Benveniste H., Kim R., Thanos P. K., Ferré S.(2012). Evidence that sleep deprivation downregulates dopamine D2R in ventral striatum in the human brain. *Journal of Neuroscience, 32*(19): 6711-6717. doi:10.1523/JNEUROSCI.0045-12.2012

Excitement

Bunzeck, N., & Düzel, E. (2006). Absolute coding of stimulus novelty in the human Substantia Nigra/VTA. *Neuron, 51*(3), 369–379. doi:10.1016/j.neuron.2006.06.021

Zald, D. H., Cowan, R. L., Riccardi, P., Baldwin, R. M., Ansari, M. S., Li, R., ... Kessler, R. M. (2008). Midbrain dopamine receptor availability is inversely associated with novelty-seeking traits in humans. *Journal of Neuroscience, 28*(53), 14372–14378. doi:10.1523/jneurosci.2423-08.2008

Positive Thinking

Ashby, F. G., Isen, A. M., & Turken, A. U. (1999). A neuropsychological theory of positive affect and its influence on cognition. *Psychological Review, 106*(3), 529–550. doi:10.1037/0033-295x.106.3.529

Barajas, Mark S. (2014). Thinking and Feeling: The Influence of Positive Emotion on Human Cognition. *The Hilltop Review, 7*(1), 3-11. Retrieved from http://scholarworks.wmich.edu/hilltopreview/vol7/iss1/3

Lövheim, H. (2012). A new three-dimensional model for emotions and monoamine neurotransmitters. *Medical Hypotheses, 78*(2), 341–348. doi:10.1016/j.mehy.2011.11.016

McMain, S., Newman, M. G., Segal, Z. V., & DeRubeis, R. J. (2015). Cognitive behavioral therapy: Current status and future research directions.

Psychotherapy Research, 25(3), 321–329.
doi:10.1080/10503307.2014.1002440

Mitchell, R. L. C., & Phillips, L. H. (2007). The psychological, neurochemical and functional neuroanatomical mediators of the effects of positive and negative mood on executive functions. *Neuropsychologia, 45*(4), 617–629. doi:10.1016/j.neuropsychologia.2006.06.030

Pressman, S. D., & Cohen, S. (2005). Does positive affect influence health? *Psychological Bulletin, 131*(6), 925–971. doi:10.1037/0033-2909.131.6.925

Sheldon, K. M., & Lyubomirsky, S. (2006). How to increase and sustain positive emotion: The effects of expressing gratitude and visualizing best possible selves. *The Journal of Positive Psychology, 1*(2), 73–82. doi:10.1080/17439760500510676

Socializing

Aragona, B. J., Liu, Y., Yu, Y. J., Curtis, J. T., Detwiler, J. M., Insel, T. R., & Wang, Z. (2005). Nucleus accumbens dopamine differentially mediates the formation and maintenance of monogamous pair bonds. *Nature Neuroscience, 9*(1), 133–139. doi:10.1038/nn1613

Carter, C. S. (1998). Neuroendocrine perspectives on social attachment and love. *Psychoneuroendocrinology, 23*(8), 779–818. doi:10.1016/s0306-4530(98)00055-9

Fordyce, M. W. (1983). A program to increase happiness: Further studies. *Journal of Counseling Psychology, 30*(4), 483-498. doi:10.1037/0022-0167.30.4.483

Insel, T. R. (2003). Is social attachment an addictive disorder? *Physiology & Behavior, 79*(3), 351–357. doi:10.1016/s0031-9384(03)00148-3

Kawachi, I. (2001). Social ties and mental health. *Journal of Urban Health: Bulletin of the New York Academy of Medicine, 78*(3), 458–467. doi:10.1093/jurban/78.3.458

Krach, S., Paulus, F. M., Bodden, M., & Kircher, T. (2010). The rewarding nature of social interactions. *Frontiers in Behavioral Neuroscience, 4*(22). doi:10.3389/fnbeh.2010.00022

Studying

McNab, F., Varrone, A., Farde, L., Jucaite, A., Bystritsky, P., Forssberg, H., & Klingberg, T. (2009). Changes in cortical dopamine D1 receptor binding associated with cognitive training. *Science, 323*(5915), 800–802. doi:10.1126/science.1166102

Riley, A. L., Zellner, D. A., & Duncan, H. J. (1980). The role of endorphins in animal learning and behavior. *Neuroscience & Biobehavioral Reviews, 4*(1), 69–76. doi:10.1016/0149-7634(80)90026-3

Sunlight

Mead, M. N. (2008). Benefits of sunlight: A bright spot for human health. *Environmental Health Perspectives, 116*(4), A160–A167. doi:10.1289/ehp.116-a160

Acupuncture

Han, J. S. (2004). Acupuncture and endorphins. *Neuroscience Letters, 361*(1-3), 258–261. doi:10.1016/j.neulet.2003.12.019

Aromatherapy

Deng, C. (2011). Aromatherapy: Exploring olfaction. *The Yale Scientific Magazine.* Retrieved from http://www.yalescientific.org/2011/11/aromatherapy-exploring-olfaction/

Warrenburg, S. (2005). Effects of fragrance on emotions: Moods and physiology. *Chemical Senses, 30*(Supplement 1), i248–i249. doi:10.1093/chemse/bjh208

Yim, V. W. C., Ng, A. K. Y., Tsang, H. W. H., & Leung, A. Y. (2009). A review on the effects of aromatherapy for patients with depressive symptoms. *The Journal of Alternative and Complementary Medicine, 15*(2), 187–195. doi:10.1089/acm.2008.0333

Pet Therapy

Beetz, A., Uvnäs-Moberg, K., Julius, H., & Kotrschal, K. (2012). Psychosocial and psychophysiological effects of human-animal interactions: the possible role of oxytocin. *Frontiers in Psychology, 3*(234). doi:10.3389/fpsyg.2012.00234

Brown, C. M., McConnell, A. R., Martin, C. E., Shoda, T. M., & Stayton, L. E. (2011). Friend with benefits: On the positive consequences of pet ownership. *Journal of Personality and Social Psychology, 101*(6), 1239-1252. doi:10.1037/a0024506

Marcus, D. A. (2013). The science behind animal-assisted therapy. *Current Pain and Headache Reports, 17*(4). doi:10.1007/s11916-013-0322-2

Odendaal, J. S. J. (2000). Animal-assisted therapy – magic or medicine? *Journal of Psychosomatic Research, 49*(4), 275–280. doi:10.1016/s0022-3999(00)00183-5

Odendaal, J. S. J., & Meintjes, R. A. (2003). Neurophysiological correlates of affiliative behaviour between humans and dogs. *The Veterinary Journal, 165*(3), 296–301. doi:10.1016/s1090-0233(02)00237-x

Smiling

Kraft, T. L., & Pressman, S. D. (2012). Grin and bear it: The influence of manipulated facial expression on the stress response. *Psychological Science, 23*(11), 1372–1378. doi:10.1177/0956797612445312

Drinking Water

Foo, H., & Mason, P. (2009). Analgesia accompanying food consumption requires ingestion of Hedonic foods. *Journal of Neuroscience, 29*(41), 13053–13062. doi:10.1523/jneurosci.3514-09.2009

Hope

See citations for the Introduction.

Compassion

Aragona, B. J., Liu, Y., Yu, Y. J., Curtis, J. T., Detwiler, J. M., Insel, T. R., & Wang, Z. (2005). Nucleus accumbens dopamine differentially mediates the formation and maintenance of monogamous pair bonds. *Nature Neuroscience, 9*(1), 133–139. doi:10.1038/nn1613

Carter, C. S. (1998). Neuroendocrine perspectives on social attachment and love. *Psychoneuroendocrinology, 23*(8), 779–818. doi:10.1016/s0306-4530(98)00055-9

Insel, T. R. (2003). Is social attachment an addictive disorder? *Physiology & Behavior, 79*(3), 351–357. doi:10.1016/s0031-9384(03)00148-3

Mathers, N. (2016). Compassion and the science of kindness: Harvard Davis Lecture 2015. *British Journal of General Practice, 66*(648), e525–e527. doi:10.3399/bjgp16x686041

Wang, S. (2005). A conceptual framework for integrating research related to the physiology of compassion and the wisdom of Buddhist teachings. In P. Gilbert (Ed.), *Compassion: Conceptualisations, research and use in psychotherapy* (pp. 121–147). London: Routledge.

Gratitude

Emmons, R. A., & McCullough, M. E. (2003). Counting blessings versus burdens: An experimental investigation of gratitude and subjective well-being in daily life. *Journal of Personality and Social Psychology, 84*(2), 377–389. doi:10.1037/0022-3514.84.2.377

McCullough, M. E., Tsang, J. A., & Emmons, R. A. (2004). Gratitude in intermediate Affective terrain: Links of grateful moods to individual differences and daily emotional experience. *Journal of Personality and Social Psychology, 86*(2), 295–309. doi:10.1037/0022-3514.86.2.295

Sheldon, K. M., & Lyubomirsky, S. (2006). How to increase and sustain positive emotion: The effects of expressing gratitude and visualizing best possible selves. *The Journal of Positive Psychology,1*(2), 73–82. doi:10.1080/17439760500510676

Courage

Laviola, G., Macrì, S., Morley-Fletcher, S., & Adriani, W. (2003). Risk-taking behavior in adolescent mice: Psychobiological determinants and early epigenetic influence. *Neuroscience & Biobehavioral Reviews, 27*(1-2), 19–31. doi:10.1016/s0149-7634(03)00006-x

Forgiveness

Worthington, E. L., Witvliet, C. V. O., Pietrini, P., & Miller, A. J. (2007). Forgiveness, health, and well-being: A review of evidence for emotional versus decisional forgiveness, dispositional forgivingness, and reduced unforgiveness. *Journal of Behavioral Medicine, 30*(4), 291–302. doi:10.1007/s10865-007-9105-8

Wrosch, C., & Renaud, J. (2011). Self-regulation of bitterness across the lifespan. In M. Linden & A. Maercker (Eds.), *Embitterment: Societal, psychological, and clinical perspectives* (pp. 129–141). Germany: Springer-Werlag Wien.

Patience

Elias, A.N., Guich, S., Wilson, A.F. (2000). Ketosis with enhanced GABAergic tone promotes physiological changes in transcendental meditation. *Medical Hypotheses, 54*(4):660-662. doi:10.1054/mehy.1999.0921

Elias, A.N. and Wilson, A.F. (1995). Serum hormonal concentrations following transcendental meditation-potential role of gamma aminobutyric acid. *Medical Hypotheses, 44*(4), 287-291. doi:10.1016/0306-9877(95)90181-7

Fonseca, M. S., Murakami, M., & Mainen, Z. F. (2015). Activation of dorsal raphe serotonergic neurons promotes waiting but is not reinforcing. *Current Biology, 25*(3), 306–315. doi:10.1016/j.cub.2014.12.002

Integrity

Crockett, M. J., Clark, L., Tabibnia, G., Lieberman, M. D., & Robbins, T. W. (2008). Serotonin modulates behavioral reactions to unfairness. *Science, 320*(5884), 1739–1739. doi:10.1126/science.1155577

Passion

Bandura, A. (1997). *Self-efficacy: The exercise of control.* United States: W. H. Freeman & Co.

O'Doherty, J. P., Deichmann, R., Critchley, H. D., & Dolan, R. J. (2002). Neural responses during anticipation of a primary taste reward. *Neuron, 33*(5), 815–826. doi:10.1016/s0896-6273(02)00603-7

Salimpoor, V. N., Benovoy, M., Larcher, K., Dagher, A., & Zatorre, R. J. (2011). Anatomically distinct dopamine release during anticipation and experience of peak emotion to music. *Nature Neuroscience, 14*(2), 257–262. doi:10.1038/nn.2726

Schott, B. H., Minuzzi, L., Krebs, R. M., Elmenhorst, D., Lang, M., Winz, O. H., ... Bauer, A. (2008). Mesolimbic functional magnetic resonance imaging activations during reward anticipation correlate with reward-related ventral striatal dopamine release. *Journal of Neuroscience, 28*(52), 14311–14319. doi:10.1523/jneurosci.2058-08.2008

Volkow, N. D., Wang, G. J., Ma, Y., Fowler, J. S., Zhu, W., Maynard, L., ... Swanson, J. M. (2003). Expectation Enhances the Regional Brain Metabolic and the Reinforcing Effects of Stimulants in Cocaine Abusers. *The Journal of Neuroscience, 23*(36), 11461–11468. Retrieved from http://www.jneurosci.org/content/23/36/11461.full.pdf

Wisdom

Jeste, D. V., & Harris, J. C. (2010). Wisdom—A Neuroscience perspective. *JAMA, 304*(14), 1602. doi:10.1001/jama.2010.1458

(Note: Multiple references from New Eyes: A Unifying Vision of Science and Spirituality)

ABOUT THE AUTHOR

STEVE TREU, LPC

is a licensed professional counselor and Chief Visionary Officer
for Quantum Revolution Inc. His insight-focused therapy uses
quantum physics to help clients understand the scientific nature
of reality, and process what it means for them from both a
physical and non-physical perspective so they can heal themselves.
As an applied quantum philosopher, Treu assists people
in exploring their infinite possibilities as they improve their
lives through a variety of mind, body and spirit techniques.

Author of *New Eyes: A Unifying Vision of Science and Spirituality.*

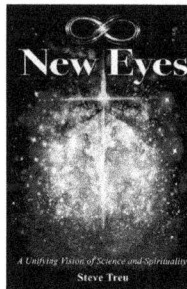

Available on amazon.com

www.ingramcontent.com/pod-product-compliance
Lightning Source LLC
Chambersburg PA
CBHW071613040426
42452CB00008B/1335